How t
Barthes' *Imag*

How to Read Theory

Series Editors:
Stephen Shapiro, Department of English and
Comparative Literary Studies, University of Warwick
Ed White, Department of English, University of Florida

How to Read Theory is a new series of clear, introductory guides to critical theory and cultural studies classics designed to encourage readers to think independently. Each title focuses on a single, key text and concisely explains its arguments and significance, showing the contemporary relevance of theory and presenting difficult theoretical concepts in clear, jargon-free prose. Presented in a compact, user-friendly format, the How to Read Theory series is designed to appeal to students and to interested readers who are coming to these key texts for the first time.

Also available:

How to Read Foucault's Discipline and Punish
Anne Schwan and Stephen Shapiro

How to Read Marx's Capital
Stephen Shapiro

How to Read
Barthes' *Image-Music-Text*

Ed White

PlutoPress
www.plutobooks.com

First published 2012 by Pluto Press
345 Archway Road, London N6 5AA

www.plutobooks.com

Distributed in the United States of America exclusively by
Palgrave Macmillan, a division of St. Martin's Press LLC,
175 Fifth Avenue, New York, NY 10010

British Library Cataloguing in Publication Data
A catalogue record for this book is available from the British Library

ISBN 978 0 7453 2958 1 Hardback
ISBN 978 0 7453 2957 4 Paperback
ISBN 978 1 8496 4722 9 PDF eBook
ISBN 978 1 8496 4724 3 Kindle eBook
ISBN 978 1 8496 4723 6 EPUB eBook

Library of Congress Cataloging in Publication Data applied for

This book is printed on paper suitable for recycling and made from
fully managed and sustained forest sources. Logging, pulping and
manufacturing processes are expected to conform to the
environmental standards of the country of origin.

10 9 8 7 6 5 4 3 2 1

Designed and produced for Pluto Press by Chase Publishing Services Ltd
Typeset from disk by Stanford DTP Services, Northampton, England
Simultaneously printed digitally by CPI Antony Rowe, Chippenham, UK and
Edwards Bros in the United States of America

Contents

Introduction   1

1. The Photographic Message   13

2. Rhetoric of the Image   25

3. The Third Meaning   38

4. Diderot, Brecht, Eisenstein   53

5. Introduction to the Structural Analysis of
   Narrative   65

6 The Struggle with the Angel   100

7. The Death of the Author   111

8. Musica Practica   122

9. From Work to Text   129

10. Change the Object Itself   139

11. Lesson in Writing   145

12. The Grain of the Voice   151

13. Writers, Intellectuals, Teachers   159

Reading Across Barthes' Work   192
Index   195

attempts to illustrate distance, movement, and change. The three thematics of its title are less guides to some Barthesian position—what Barthes concluded about images, for example—than fields in which Barthes worked out larger problems of language and interpretation. What this means for today's reader of *Image-Music-Text* is that the collection is best approached not as an assemblage of position papers but as an entry point to certain problems that characterize Barthes and his tremendous influence. While anthologies of literary theory may reprint "The Death of the Author" as the paradigmatic Barthesian critical statement, it is more helpful to see it as one essay in a series, Barthes at work trying to address a particular set of problems and to open up a new set of solutions. *How to Read Image-Music-Text* attempts to be such a guide, helping new readers of Barthes appreciate the stakes, revisions, aims, and above all *process* of the various arguments of the collection.

What this means for you, as you read *Image-Music-Text*, is that you are not seeing a critic's set positions so much as following the arcs of his writing, and I would highlight three worth tracing. The first and most obvious is Barthes' changing positions on language, which he initially views as a system of meaning veiling reality, but increasingly comes to see as the very environment of humans comprised of both repressive elements *and* emancipatory potential. The latter he increasingly finds in "writing" as an activity, and the essays of *Image-Music-Text* can be read as Barthes' path to becoming an exponent of that particular political attitude about language. This is a second arc that might be traced: Barthes was always friendly to radical politics, and his earliest works are typically marxist, if also contrarian, challenging orthodox positions of the Left. His critiques of leftist assumptions accelerated through the 1960s, producing a very different sense of the intellectual engaged in political change. The last essay in this collection, "Writers, Intellectuals, Teachers" (1971), demonstrates some of these shifts, though it also shows Barthes still very much interested in the marxist project. I have not offered much commentary on this political change, though I have tried to highlight how it mutates. Some have argued that Barthes' political journey offers a needed clarity and modernization of marxism, while others suggest that we see a weakening of his politics with his institutional success. I leave that verdict for readers to determine. The third arc I would mention here concerns the dramatic changes in Barthes' style. His earliest essays are very methodical, scientistic in tone, and focused on particular research problems. In the mid to late 1960s, however, we begin to see manifestos that are more calls to new ways of thinking than detailed arguments in the older sense. The last essay in the collection is openly experimental and fragmentary, not to mention contradictory: it is more an attempt to write out the process of thinking through several problems than it is a didactic essay with a clear message. These varying styles are among the pleasures and challenges of reading *Image-Music-Text*, and are best read as indications of Barthes' changing positions on language itself. He adopts different styles of writing in part to demonstrate his claims.

On a still larger scale, a reading of Barthes' development as a thinker—how he framed problems of analysis, then revised them—will provide readers with a point of access to the larger critical movement known as poststructuralism. François Dosse, in his two volume *History of Structuralism*, has written a long and detailed history of structuralism *and* poststructuralism that usefully recounts the foundational influence of structuralist linguistics and anthropology upon a range of creative and active theorists, including Michel Foucault (1926-1984), Jacques Derrida (1930-2004), Jacques Lacan (1901-1981), Julia Kristeva (1941-), and Barthes (1915-1980)—all names students regularly encounter today in footnotes, if not through their original essays. Many of these theorists were strongly committed to a progressive analysis of modern capitalist society through the particular lens of language, viewed as society's most important structure and form. Barthes was certainly among this number. If poststructuralist ideas and theories increasingly expressed pessimism about social change, a study of their development will help us see both the insights and the shortcomings of such a project—in other words, not only the insights but the limitations of cultural analysis through the sign.

Before turning to the essays of *Image-Music-Text*, however, it will help to understand Barthes' rise to prominence in the late 1950s, particularly with his book *Mythologies*. In the mid-1950s, Barthes had written short interpretive essays—the "mythologies"—mostly for the journal *Les Lettres Nouvelles*. These pieces were among the first popular examples of what might today be called "cultural studies." In generally non-specialized language, Barthes interpreted such popular media phenomena as sensational criminal trials, movie posters and acting styles, advertisements, and iconic humanitarians. He analyzed tour books, science-fiction heroes and aliens, automobile design, and the norms of cooking lay-outs in women's magazines. He discussed sporting events, children's toys, Einstein's intelligence, and natural history museums. He treated wine and milk, steak and fries, plastic and wood, the U.S. preacher Billy Graham and the French striptease. In many of the pieces, he addressed French cultural politics, from the conservatism of book reviews to forms of racism, from the rationales for imperial interventions in Africa to the neo-fascist rightwing parties and their spokesmen. (The 1972 English translation removed many of the more overtly political essays, giving a slightly misleading sense of Barthes' project.) In 1957, these mythologies were gathered together and published in book form; at the end, Barthes included a long essay entitled "Myth Today," in which he attempted to describe what he had been doing in more theoretical terms. That essay requires a brief explication, for in it, Barthes began his more sustained engagement with French structuralism, the language of which runs through the essays of *Image-Music-Text*.

Barthes begins by stressing that what he is calling mythology is not defined by its subject matter but is rather a *"type of speech,"* a *"form"* of communication (109). Everything can be potentially mythologized, and there are no eternal myths across time—rather, mythologizing, as a "mode of signification," exists across time, and should be studied as part of "semiology," or the "science of forms" (111). We should appreciate this gesture, about which Barthes shows a bit of defensiveness. As we see later, Barthes was very sympathetic to various forms of marxism in postwar France, and some of his contemporary communists and marxists would have condemned this interest in form as apolitical or downright conservative—one should not be talking abstractly about how mythology works, they might argue, but rather examining the historical content and details of such myths. To such criticisms, Barthes responds with a famous reworking of a statement by Lenin: "I shall say that a little formalism turns one away from History, but that a lot brings one back to it" (112). We will see shortly how Barthes argues that form can be political and historical.

Inspired by the Swiss linguist Ferdinand de Saussure, Barthes spells out one of the basic claims of "semiology": everything that signifies, that has or communicates meaning, has a "tri-dimensional" structure of "the signifier, the signified and the sign" (114). We may illustrate this with a simple, non-verbal example: a bunch of roses that "I use...to *signify* my passion" (113). The bunch of roses is the signifier, and my passion is the signified. From a naive point of view, the relationship between roses and passion is natural and timeless, but in reality it is not—roses might mean any number of things at different historical moments or different cultural contexts, and for some people may represent the commercial flower industry, greenhouses, Valentine's Day gifts, adolescent forms of dating, an allergy, and so on. The specific association of the signifier (a bunch of roses) and the signified (my passion) is thus not obvious or eternal, but a specific relationship called a "sign." The term is important to stress that relationship between different things, and Barthes proceeds to give a different example from the field of psychoanalysis. Sigmund Freud, in his analysis of dreams, distinguished between the "manifest datum" of a dream and the dream's "latent content." Let's say that I dream that I am falling from an airplane (the manifest datum) and that my dream is about my anxiety that I will miss my first day at work (the latent content): the dream in this case is the sign, the relationship between the signifier and the signified. Identifying this third term is important because it shows that the relationship between signifier and signified is not "natural" or "normal," but rather historical and social.

What then is the myth? According to Barthes, it is a *"second-order semiological system,"* a kind of *"metalanguage"* about language. Mythology, as a form of communication, takes a sign as its signifier, links it with a more complex signified, and produces a second-order sign, which Barthes calls a "signification." In the diagram below, Arabic numerals depict the terms of the first-order sign, while Roman numerals depict the second order signification of myth.

1. Signifier	3. Sign	III. SIGN (signification)
2. Signified	I. SIGNIFIER	
	II. SIGNIFIED	

Barthes proceeds to give a few examples of what he is describing. In the first example, a student studying Latin in school encounters the phrase "quia ego nominor leo" in her textbook. Literally, this translates as "because my name is lion." But this phrase, taken out of context, will be recognized by the student as something else—"a grammatical example meant to illustrate the rule about the agreement of the predicate" (116). In this example, the assembled words are a first-order signifier, and "because my name is lion" is the first-order signified: the relationship between the Latin phrase and my translation of it is the first-order sign. But in the context of my grammar book, that sign becomes a second-order signifier of a second-order signified (the grammatical rule I am supposed to learn), and is therefore a second-order sign as well.

Why this might matter will be clearer with Barthes' second example, the image on the cover of the popular French magazine, *Paris-Match* (issue 326, July 1955). The cover depicts an adolescent black boy in a military uniform, his hand in the gesture of a salute, his eyes looking in the distance, apparently at the French flag. The message of the magazine cover is clear to the French viewer: that France is great, that black subjects of French imperialism serve faithfully and with zeal, that therefore the French colonial system functions effectively and justly. In a first-order interpretation, we might see this as just a picture of a young black soldier or scout making a salute, and we might try to imagine the possible contexts or different meanings of the picture. But here, on the cover of *Paris-Match*, any complex account of this photograph, any exploration of its context, suddenly evaporates—"it empties itself, it becomes impoverished, history evaporates, only the letter remains" (117). Emptied of historical, contextual complexity, the first-order sign becomes a signifier of a second-order signification—a black soldier saluting in a moment of history becomes an abstraction.

Barthes has thus explained three concurrent dynamics. First, he has shown how some signs acquire meaning. In his examples, the myth, or second-order sign, gains its signification from a first-order sign: the Latin phrase is removed from its original textual context, and becomes a grammatical example, or the saluting black adolescent becomes an illustration of the soundness of French imperialism. But he has also shown how some signs *lose* meaning, and become "impoverished" (120). For the first-order sign is, as myth, stripped of its first-order meaning: the Latin phrase is removed from its context, as is the black adolescent. However, what makes the myth particularly effective is its doubleness. The first-order sign oscillates back and forth with meaning—now it is sign, now it is signifier—as if in a "turnstile" (123). Barthes also gives the example here of a train passenger looking out the train window: at one moment, she watches the details of the landscape, but at another moment, she focuses on the window pane itself, as all the details of the landscape become blurry (123). This oscillation of perspective is important because it allows for an "alibi" to be built into the second-order sign, the myth. If I object to the magazine cover, and complain that this is a picture designed to defend and support French imperialism, the defender of the myth will answer that she has no idea what I am talking about—this is just a photograph of a black adolescent making a salute. To take another example: in the 1988 presidential election in the United States, the George H. W. Bush campaign produced an advertisement against the Democratic candidate, former Massachusetts governor Michael Dukakis. Dukakis had supported a reformative furlough program for prisoners in Massachusetts, during which program several prisoners fled and committed crimes. The Bush campaign chose to run a campaign spot featuring several pictures of William Horton, an African-American prisoner who had committed murder and rape while in the furlough program. Many observers of the ad criticized it as racist because of its choice of example and the way the images were presented (Horton was labeled "Willie," depicted with a large afro, and framed in several images to emphasize his large size). In Barthes' terms, they were criticizing the second-order, mythic meaning of the advertisement. The response from the Bush campaign was to appeal to the first-order sign: in other words, they shifted perspective, or went through the turnstile, to insist that this was only the picture of one person who had committed crimes while on the furlough program. Any broader meaning, they added, was being imposed on the ad, and was not intentional. This turnstile alibi was possible because the Willie Horton ad functioned as a myth, a sign on two different levels, a "double system" (123).

The theoretical focus of the "Myth Today" essay is this reading of myth as second-order sign, as a form of "language-robbery" (131) that strips history from language, and "transforms history into nature" (129). Barthes discusses myth's "imperative, button-holing character" (124)—the ways it imposes itself upon subjects—as well as its socio-historical foundations. He argues that myth is the preferred mode of language for any bourgeois society, for the bourgeoisie wants to cast its views, beliefs, and practices as timeless and universal, and erase the historical contingencies that led to and maintain its rule. If the ideal model of a wedding ceremony is that of the big ritual of ostentatious consumption—elaborate clothing worn one time, expenditures on ephemeral decorations, the gift of the precious stone—this is so because of mythology, whereby a very specific bourgeois practice has been stripped of its history to become the natural norm for the working class as well (141). If one feels awkward using seemingly old-fashioned, marxist class language—like "the bourgeoisie"—this is no accident: "it is the bourgeois ideology itself, the process through which the bourgeoisie transforms the reality of the world into an image of the world, History into Nature" (141). Once language is stripped of history and rendered "natural" or "universal," our political view of our social world is itself stripped away: myth, in other words, is *"depoliticized speech"* (143).

Consequently, to regain a sense of political struggle, to be fully a part of history, one must determine a strategy to counter the ubiquity of myth. To clarify this struggle, Barthes identifies three positions in relation to myth: the producer (for example, an advertiser or a journalist) who willingly produces the myth; the "mythologist" who, like Barthes, debunks or "deciphers" the myth; and the consumer or reader of myths, who passively responds according to the producer's motivations (128). Of these three positions, it clearly seems preferable to be a mythologist or debunker, but in the concluding section of the essay, subtitled "Necessity and limits of mythology," Barthes adds a troubling note. For there are, for the mythologist, "a few difficulties" (156). Let us imagine an unrelentingly debunking mythologist, constantly stripping away the illusory second-order signs. This mythologist thereby distances herself "from all the myth-consumers," meaning she may be "estranged" from both the "public" but also the "very object of the myth" (157). If the mythologist debunks the myth of French wine, perhaps the pleasure of wine will disappear. Earlier, Barthes had offered a suggestion for vanquishing myth—creating a third-order sign or second-order myth, an "artificial myth" that would build upon the myth itself. "Since myth robs language of something, why not rob myth," he asks, and he gives the example of the French writer Gustave Flaubert's novel *Bouvard and Pécuchet*, in which the two title characters—both bourgeois to the extreme—are comically depicted attempting to pursue various bourgeois myths and behaviors, always with disappointing results (135). Bourgeois myths are themselves mythologized. To take the example given earlier, the racist "Willie Horton" campaign advertisement, many critics have referred to that advertisement so frequently—as a paradigmatic racist ad—that it has achieved the status of what Barthes calls an "artificial myth." The problem with this strategy, or so Barthes argues at the end of his essay, is that the mythologist becomes increasingly remote from both the language of the working-class and from the world itself. This deep state of alienation from our world signals not only "an unstable grasp of reality" but also an inability to appreciate the "wholeness" of the world. If we analyze the language that constitutes the world, we "liberate it but we destroy it"—that is, we end the reign of myth but lose our grasp on that reality at the same time. And if we acknowledge the myth, we unwittingly "restore it" to its mystification (159). This "split in the social world" caused by language is the final problem asserted in *Mythologies*, the final sentence of which reads: "And yet, this is what we must seek: a reconciliation between reality and men [sic], between description and explanation, between object and knowledge" (158). It is this reconciliation, in the sphere of photography, that Barthes addresses in the first essay of *Image-Music-Text*.

A final note on the gendered language of Barthes' writing: like many of his contemporaries, Barthes consistently uses the male pronoun, in part as a default of French, in part because he rarely addresses women artists or imagines women as teachers or writers. I have tried to correct or modify this use of the masculine pronoun throughout my treatment of his essays.

1. The Photographic Message

This essay, the earliest included in *Image-Music-Text*, seems to take as its primary concern the isolation and characterization of the photograph—specifically the *press* photograph—as a unique medium for communication. Barthes had earlier analyzed many photographic images—glamour shots of Greta Garbo and Audrey Hepburn, for example, or the *Paris-Match* cover—but here he treats the press shot specifically as an image, and specifically the kind of image created by a camera. The photograph as a unique technological medium was a subject of interest to Barthes throughout his career—he included personal photographs in his autobiography, *Roland Barthes*, and one of his last books, *Camera Lucida*, explores the photograph and what it means. But as Barthes will eventually indicate, his project is more profound: he wants to address the problem of how—or if—we can perceive and access the objective reality of the world around us. Hence his choice of the press photograph, rather than, say, the artistic photograph or (the focus of the next essay) the advertisement photograph: the press photograph, Barthes insists, seems unique among forms of communication, and accentuates a particular theoretical problem unique to photographic technology.

Barthes begins, characteristically, by clearing the field of related but nonetheless distinct questions. The first paragraph raises the complex system of "emission," "transmission," and "reception" for any press photograph (15). In assessing the press photograph, one would presumably consider the staff of the newspaper (the photographer herself, the technicians in the lay-out department, the editors, and so on), the demographics of the particular newspaper (the class background and political affiliation of its readers, for example). These matters of emission and reception, however, belong to a separate field of study—the sociological analysis of a mass medium—distinct from the problem of "the message itself" (15). Even after we understand the workings of the newspaper, the fact remains that the press photograph "is not simply a product or a channel but also *an object endowed with a structural autonomy*" (15, emphasis added). Consequently, our analysis needs to be suited to its "unique structure," and should be able to distinguish analytically those other sociological elements (16). Barthes reiterates this point in talking about the photograph's transmission, which will always involve an accompanying text—the caption or title, the accompanying article. Yes, this textual material and the photographic image "are co-operative," and work in tandem, but nonetheless, they are different kinds of messages. We must carefully distinguish these types of messages for a number of reasons. For one thing, we already have some understanding of how written language works. As a result, we will tend to give that analysis of words greater importance in our interpretation of the photograph, the workings of which we have yet to appreciate and understand. Distinguishing these different types of signification is therefore particularly important because "only when the study of each structure has been exhausted" will it "be possible to understand the manner in which they complement one another" (16).

If the photograph is a different kind of sign than words, what exactly is it? What makes the photograph unique, Barthes claims, is that unlike other kinds of messages, it transmits "the literal reality" that it has technologically captured (17). Of course the image is not reality, but it *is* a "perfect *analogon*...it is exactly this analogical perfection which, to common sense, defines the photograph" (17). By contrast, other forms of representation will "divide up this reality into units," then "constitute these units as signs" of a different mode than that which they represent (17). A written description of a street demonstration, for example, will utilize a series of words that translate the actual scene according to the rules of writing; a drawing of the demonstration will highlight certain elements and use techniques available to that particular art form. In both cases, a linguistic "code" will be evident—the code of words, the code of sketching—and interpreters will necessarily encounter the "relay" set up by that code. To be sure, the photograph of the street demonstration is not the same thing as the demonstration and will not be a complete representation: it will not capture all the visual elements or perspectives, or the non-visual sensations (what it feels like to be in the crowd, the motivations of the demonstrators, etc.). But it is nonetheless, by virtue of its technological process, an analogon of that demonstration. Thus the "special status" of the photograph, according to Barthes: *"it is a message without a code"* (17).

Barthes quickly adds what he considers to be an important corollary: "the photographic message is a continuous message" (17). The photograph is continuous—constant in time, without a beginning or an end—precisely because it lacks a code. A code would give the interpretation a specific temporal sequence. The written description of the street demonstration must be written and read in some syntactic sequence, from beginning to end, and it is that process that marks the beginning and end of the interpretive encounter with writing. What about other visual or analogical forms of representation, like "drawings, paintings, cinema, [or] theatre"? These other forms all involve some "obvious" form of additional message "supplementary" to the analogous element. The clearest example would be the stylistic elements of the reproduction. In the case of the drawing of the demonstration, the style or the coloring of the drawing will draw on artistic conventions to convey an additional or supplemental message: harsh lines and shading, for example, might be used to emphasize anger or danger. Even the attempt to give a completely neutral and "realistic" drawing will be recognized as a certain kind of artistic style—for example, "verism" (18). To give another example, we are very aware of this encoding when we watch a documentary: we recognize certain elements of filming (say, perspective and texture) and the sequential presentation of information as part of the documentarian's "code." Barthes concludes that these other artistic modes, despite being "imitative" or representational, all "comprise two messages: a *denoted* message, which is the *analogon* itself, and a *connoted* message, which is the manner in which the society to a certain extent communicates what it thinks of it" (17).

Denotation and connotation will be terms that Barthes employs repeatedly throughout the essays of *Image-Music-Text*. Denotation, as Barthes uses the term, refers to a neutral or what some would call "objective" designation or indication of that which is represented: Barthes later calls this a "first-order message" (18). Connotation, by contrast, refers to the abstract or "subjective" interpretive elements, which are the substance (or "second-order message") of most of our interpretations (18). A still-life painting—let's say, of a plate, some vegetables, a fish, and a knife—at the most simple level denotes those objects portrayed, but it may also, depending on its context and presentation, *connote* nourishment, commodities, the simple pleasures of a fishing community, the labor of gathering and preparing food, or the elegant pleasures of bourgeois feasting. Connotation is thus the realm of interpretation in which cultural, historical values are layered upon the denoted elements. If we return to the model of the sign discussed in the introduction, we may say that the signifier here corresponds to denotation, while the signified corresponds to connotation.

Signifier (denotation)	Sign (relationship of denotation to connotation)
Signified (connotation)	

Barthes finds the press photograph worthy of analysis because, at first glance, it "appears" to be purely denotative, a simple "mechanical analogue of reality," in which the denotation "fills" our interpretation and "leaves no place" for connotation. Such is our "common sense" perception of the photograph—it captures what was actually *there* at some point in time. In fact, the press photograph "has been worked on, chosen, composed, constructed, treated according to professional, aesthetic or ideological norms which are so many factors of connotation" (19). We should try to understand how this code works, appreciating what is unique about the press photograph. It is not like the other signs that Barthes has mentioned (film, drawings, paintings, theater) because with those forms, connotation does not work in "collusion" with denotation. With the drawing, the very elements of its composition (lines, shading, color, etc.) are working simultaneously to denote and connote.

With the press photograph, connotation occurs apart from the denotation—or, as Barthes puts it, "the connoted (or coded) message develops on the basis of a message *without a code*" (19). Barthes is thus arguing a corollary of the Saussurean argument about the sign. Remember that according to Saussure, the relationship between the signifier and the signified is not natural or inevitable (these roses will not always signify my passion). When we speak of that relationship, we are *describing* how signifier and signified are linked, but we are not claiming that this relationship is necessary. Here Barthes is making a very similar argument about connotation and denotation in relation to the press photograph:

Denotation (analogon of photographed object)	
Connotation (interpretation)	Press photograph

The puzzle here is how and why specific connotations become associated with a specific denotation in the thing we call the press photograph. More broadly, it is clear that Barthes is asking why and how specific signifieds become associated with specific signifiers in the things we call signs—and he is using the press photograph to explore this problem.

If this puzzle seems esoteric, Barthes explains the larger issues at stake in his project. The structure he describes with the press photograph finds a parallel in "an ethical paradox": when one tries to be ethical, one strives to be as "neutral" or "objective" as possible, "as though the analogical were a factor of resistance against the investment of values" (19-20). Is this ethical neutrality possible? Barthes' gambit here is that his analysis of the interpretation of the press photograph will shed some light on this larger problem.

At this point, Barthes turns to the "connotation procedures" and elements that are imposed upon the press photograph, and thereby amount to "a coding of the photographic analogue" (20). "[S]trictly speaking," the procedures Barthes goes on to explain, are *not* "part of the photographic structure" (20). The visual techniques are divided in two categories. First are those procedures which modify the photographic analogon. "Trick effects"—what we today call "photoshopping"—involves the faking of an image by inserting elements already "heavily connoted" (21). (Barthes' example here is a famous photograph of Senator Millard Tydings; the notorious anti-Communist Joseph McCarthy, who had been investigated by Tydings, had faked a photograph depicting Tydings' meeting with the U.S. Communist leader Earl Browder.) Posing also comprises an "'historical grammar'" of connotation. For example, the famous 1960 portrait of John F. Kennedy, by the Canadian Yousuf Karsh, connotes "youthfulness, spirituality, [and] purity" (22). The arrangement of objects is another connotative technique, as many objects are already laden with meaning (a book-case connotes intellectuality, the gas-chamber door evokes a long mythological tradition of the gates of death, and so on). If the first three procedures involve the objects photographed, three other procedures are concerned, rather, with the presentation of the photograph itself. "Photogenia" is the embellishment of the photograph through, for example, alterations of lighting, exposure, printing, and blurring. In addition to these "aesthetic *effects*," some photographs deploy a more direct imitation of, or allusion to, aesthetic techniques (23-24). For instance,

Henri Cartier-Bresson's 1938 "Cardinal Pacelli," one of Barthes' examples, duplicates the iconographic framing of much older European traditions of painting. Finally, photographic syntax or sequence adds a temporal, narrative connotation. Barthes' example here is a 1950 series of four photographs by Dmitri Kessel for *Life* magazine, portraying French President Vincent Auriol shooting a hunting rifle as his aides duck and bob to avoid getting shot: one of the photographs might suggest an awkward situation, but the four together connote a slapstick scene of danger.

All of these photographic modifications amount to instances of connotation trying to impose itself on denotation, to overwhelm it. And we find something similar in the words that often accompany the press photograph—the textual caption. When text and image traditionally appeared alongside one another (say, in the nineteenth century), the image clarified or connoted the written word: hence the term "illustration." If I am describing geological sedimentation, I will include an illustration (say, a cross-section of rock) to demonstrate what my words are describing. But in an "historical reversal," the text is now (as Barthes writes in the late twentieth century) "parasitic" upon the image (25). What Barthes means is that the text now provides connotation for the image, and in so doing undermines the image by "burdening it with a culture, a moral, an imagination" (26). This added connotation may be close to the connotations already visually ascribed to the photograph, or it may invent new meanings, or it may even contradict the already-present connotation (27). In fact, it is "impossible" that the words "duplicate" or correspond in some way to the meaning of the image (26)—after all, the two are different kinds of sign systems, with different structures and logics. Nonetheless, the textual connotation is "experienced...as the natural resonance" of the image's denotation: the cultural content of the connotation is naturalized, by virtue of the new relationship between text and image (26).

What does Barthes conclude from this analysis? With the photograph, there is no such thing as a natural or "trans-historical" interpretation. There will always be connotation through a process of "signification," the inevitable perception of meaning (27), or, to put it more bluntly, connotation will always overwhelm denotation. And this means that "the reading of the photograph is thus always historical" (28). The long process of this essay—finding all the elements that add connotation to the press photograph—has resulted in finding nothing but its own powerful inventory, which likely says more about "the reader's cultural situation" than some elusive reality captured by photography (28). Instead of trying to strip away connotation, one should accept, following the work of such psychologists as Jerome Bruner and Jean Piaget, that "there is no perception without immediate categorization" (28). There may be one exception to this rule—the experience of trauma, defined here as the blocking of categories and concepts—but this is a rarity (28). As a rule, the image "has *no denoted state, is immersed for its very social existence in at least an initial layer of connotation*" (29, emphasis added). Again it may be helpful to think about this argument relative to the model of the sign:

Analagon (denotation) *signifier*	⬆	Press photo
Interpretation (connotation) *signified*		*sign*

The argument here is that, with the press photograph, the connotation—that which is signified—overwhelms the denotation—the analogous depiction of the photograph—more or less completely. Remember here the common-sense understanding of the sign: we typically think that the signifier (a rose) has some intrinsic or natural meaning (love, passion), and thus that the sign describes the dominance of the signifier over the signified. The Saussurean or structuralist analysis answered, No, the relationship between signifier and signified is not inevitable, but is instead contingent: the sign describes that contingent linkage between signifier and signified. But here Barthes offers a different understanding of that relationship, at least as it plays out in the press photograph: not only is the signifier-signified relationship contingent, but it may be the case that the signified dramatically dominates the signifier.

So how does this overwhelming connotation—the priority of signified over signifier—occur? It may be the case that a first process of "perceptive connotation" takes place, isolating certain signifiers within the photographic analogon. A second and more complex stage might be "cognitive connotation," whereby the reader or viewer seeks out "the greatest possible quantity of information" in a search for clarity (29). A third stage might then be some kind of ideological or ethical connotation (29-30). However this connotation happens as a mental process, it is clear that the image itself has no inherent political or ideological meaning. "[N]o photograph has ever convinced or refuted anyone" (30), and the same image can be interpreted to suit one's views: one could give a "right-wing reading or a left-wing reading" to any image (30), because that reading is not part of the denotation (inherent in the image) but comes from the connotative interpretation.

If "connotation extends a long way," intruding upon denotation, does this mean "a pure denotation, a *this-side of language*, is impossible?" (30). In other words, is there ever a case where we could look at a press photo and access what it depicts or captures? Barthes here briefly mentions a linguistic category—the neutral, whereby connotation is extremely weak or barely existent—only to dismiss it as a possibility (30). Instead, he asserts that the only such case one can imagine is trauma—the "suspension of language" or "blocking of meaning" (30). When someone experiences trauma, according to this argument drawn from Freud, the problem is not that she has experienced something with horrible, awful connotations (like an act of violence), but rather that the experience is so powerful as to *defy* connotation—it literally cannot be signified, it makes no sense. This is why Barthes argues that "the shock-photo is by structure insignificant" (31), because it has no significance. As a result, the "'mythological' effect of a photograph is inversely proportional to its traumatic effect" (31): the more traumatic it is, the less connotative it will be, the less traumatic it is, the more connotative the photograph will be. In any case, trauma is neither desirable nor common, and is mentioned here not as an ideal—a way to get to pure denotation—but to illustrate the near-impossibility of such a goal.

Barthes finally concludes his essay with some conclusions from this test case. He has concluded that this form of communication, which we normally consider "the unculture of a 'mechanical' art"—something free of social meaning—is in fact "the most social of institutions" (31). While this may be a bleak conclusion—we do not (at least with the press photograph) have access to "the way things are"—Barthes identifies what may be the analytical silver lining of this discovery. The relentless process of photographic connotation is "an institutional activity," whose "function is to integrate man, to reassure him" (31). What this means, speaking more generally, is that this connotative process describes not simply how human interpretations are directed or manipulated, but more fundamentally how humans fit into their respective societies. Here Barthes mentions G. W. F. Hegel's analysis of Greek culture in which he explained the Greeks "by outlining the manner in which they made nature signify," instead of what one might expect—a descriptive catalogue of "the totality of their 'feelings and beliefs'" (31). In simpler terms, we understand society better if we understand *how* meaning happens rather than *which* meanings result. Thus this study of the photograph as a structure helps us figure out how its "codes" work—a tougher task than summing up the content of these codes. This is the critical task with which Barthes concludes his essay. By "trying to reconstitute in its specific structure the code of connotation," we may find "the forms our society uses to ensure its peace of mind and to grasp thereby, the magnitude, the detours and the underlying function of that activity" (31). These three qualities are important. "Magnitude" stresses the tremendous, almost universal range of forms. The "detours" reveal how indirect these forms may work—in this case, connotation both imposes upon and draws away from the potential of denotation, so that what seems straightforwardly real is actually nothing but connotation. Finally, the "underlying function" describes the ends for which such means work. In sum, the meaning of form is more important than its content, for form is where we locate the full range and dynamics of social power.

2. Rhetoric of the Image

"The Photographic Message" appeared in the premier issue of the French journal *Communications* in 1961. For the next few years, Barthes reviewed several studies of the image in the pages of this same journal, and in 1964 published "Rhetoric of the Image." This new essay is still interested in the question of the image as a sign—as a relationship between signifier and signified—and as he begins this essay, Barthes stresses the paradoxical status of the image. On the one hand, some people view the image as very rudimentary and basic—a picture lacks the complexity and nuance of written language, for example, and seems crude alongside something like a poem. By this view, the image is something that *resists* meaning, as when we say that it is difficult to describe something that we have seen. On the other hand, the image is often understood as being so much more complex and rich than written language. This is often expressed in the sentiment that "a picture is worth a thousand words," or the sense that a photograph brings a situation to life in ways a verbal or written description cannot. Because of this paradoxical status—the image is empty of meaning, the image is full of meaning—we can explore the image to better understand the "ontology of the process of signification" (32), that is, we can see how the process of meaning works and exists. These basic questions—"How does meaning get into the image? Where does it end? And if it ends, what is there *beyond*?"—are all considered here, though in unexpected ways. For one thing, Barthes changes his choice of image. His 1961 essay examined the newspaper photograph (the image of what seems to be the "real world" of the event) as an example of an image that *should*, according to common sense, most resist connotation. Here, however, Barthes reverses this framework, turning to the advertising image. Why? Again, in our common-sense view, we imagine it to be the most contrived and manipulated of all images. As Barthes understates the matter, the advertisement is "undoubtedly intentional," "*frank*, or at least emphatic" (33). In contrast to the press photograph, which Barthes characterized as the conjunction of a weak signifier and a strong signified, the advertisement photograph joins the strong signifier with a weaker signified. With this very different choice, we will see Barthes work through a similar process of analysis.

His specific choice of image is an advertisement for Panzani foods (see image XVII facing page 53), which was to become one of the major French marketers of Mediterranean and especially Italian food. In looking at this simple advertisement, Barthes begins by identifying three different kinds of messages. The first is a *linguistic* message, found in the caption and the product labels. Some of these linguistic terms are clearly denotational—"sauces" obviously describes what one of the products is—but they may also be connotational. *Panzani*, for instance, denotes the name of the company, but from the sound of the word, the concluding vowel, and the letter *z*, it also signifies for French readers the Italian dimensions of the food (33).

Barthes calls the second type of message a "coded iconic message" (36) or a "symbolic" message (37). With the Panzani advertisement, Barthes identifies at least four different symbolic encodings. One might see a scene representing "a return from the market," with its associations of fresh produce and home cooking; one might see "Italianicity" in the ways the photograph draws on French tourist stereotypes (for example, the color scheme of the ad, or the association of the combination of vegetables); on a more commercial level, one might see here "the idea of a total culinary service" through which one company provides all one needs for a pleasant meal; and finally, one might see here echoes of the artistic genre of the still life, composed of commodities, tools, and natural objects (34-35). Barthes lists these four symbolic encodings not to provide an exhaustive account of the photograph, but to illustrate how the iconic message may be encoded. These four codes are "discontinuous" (34) and "require a generally cultural knowledge" (35)—if a viewer is unfamiliar with the still life genre, or with the cultural history of French perceptions of Italy, she might not perceive these encodings, and even if she is, these four codes will not necessarily come together neatly.

What Barthes has described, in these two kinds of messages, are the same two sources of connotation described in "The Photographic Message"—the (parasitic) text and the connotative associations of the image. But Barthes now turns to a third message inherent in the Panzani ad—the "non-coded iconic message" which he also calls the "literal message" (36). This "literal message" is that the pasta package, the net, the cans of sauce, and so on, all existed somewhere when they were photographed. This third message—these things are—is described by Barthes as "quasi-tautological" (36), almost like asserting that A=A. This kind of message requires background knowledge—we need to be old enough to know what an image is, and we need to know what the basic things photographed are—but we do not need to be familiar with any of the symbolic codes (Italianicity, the still life, etc.); we need what Barthes calls "almost anthropological knowledge," basic knowledge of human society.

Barthes anticipates several objections to this identification of the third, non-coded iconic message. For one thing, how can one distinguish this simpler message from the elaborate, multiform coded iconic message? Barthes answers that, while in our lived experience, we may not be able to separate the two message forms, the analytical distinction is still important, and may lead to a better understanding of how the image works. The project of the essay, after all, is to get a "structural description" of the "inter-relationship of the three messages" (37). There is another possible objection: what does this weak, non-coded iconic message matter? After all, it doesn't seem like much of a message. Barthes gives his thesis in response: "the literal message appears as the *support* of the 'symbolic message'" (37). We will eventually see what Barthes means by this, but first he revisits the three kinds of messages to explore in more detail how they work.

So Barthes returns to the linguistic message. Does a textual message always accompany an image? While we may be able to imagine a society of images without words, this is really an historical question. At the present moment (1964)—a moment declared to be "a civilization of the image"—written texts still dominate images, even when images are everywhere and textual notation minimal. For no matter how short it may be, the written message "counts...thanks to connotations" (38). What does the written message do? It has one or both of two functions:

"*anchorage* and *relay*" (38). The image is "polysemous"—containing multiple semes, or signifying elements—such that for any image there is a "'floating chain' of signifieds" (39) from which viewers may choose. Every society develops techniques to deal with polysemy, to make signs more stable, and the linguistic message is one of these. If I see an image and cannot get my bearings—that is, if I am considering all the possible meanings I may give to the image—the text gives me an anchoring point, even if that answer is often incomplete. Imagine a picture of a mountain panorama, through which winds a highway with a lone car. If the caption of this picture reads "Switzerland," I may instantly sort the picture's codes as a tourist promotion (if one visits Switzerland, one can move about on the highways among the amazing scenery); if the caption reads "Mercedes," I may sort the codes as an auto advertisement (the car comes from the rugged mountains of Europe, or is perfect for challenging driving conditions, etc.); if the caption reads "007," I may sort the codes and see the image as a still from a James Bond adventure movie; and so on. The linguistic anchor thus helps me "to choose *the correct level of perception*," and acts like a "vice which holds the connoted meanings from proliferating" or going in the wrong direction (39). Sometimes this anchorage must be conceived as a form of "*dispatching*," or a form of remote control, as when a linguistic anchor prepares the viewer of the image for an eventual message (40). In all of these cases, the anchorage is a form of selective, directed control. If there is some kind of "elucidation" that comes from the written text, we must recognize that it is partial, and just as important for excluding different interpretations of the image. Therefore, anchorage is a *"repressive"* phenomenon, restricting and suppressing the possible interpretations of the sign (40).

The other function of the written text described by Barthes is that of "relay," most evident in comic strips or films. In comic strips, we might find a series of framed images, with small amounts of text (e.g., dialogue between characters presented in speech or thought bubbles) which direct the interpretation of the images. In these cases, the text moves along perception not so much by ordering one's interpretation of the individual comic strip blocks but by moving the reader quickly through the sequence. That is, one does not fill out one's reading of the individual image in a strong sense, for the two sign systems—the drawings and the text—move along as complementary. In such cases, the image provides a weak support for the written text. Imagine the punchline of a comic strip sequence, in which the illustration presents a character with a few question marks around its head, indicating confusion or surprise; in this case, the image adds a detail about how to interpret the text (the punchline evokes a comic confusion in one of the characters), though the image (probably of a stock character appearing in all the comic strips) otherwise adds little. In the case of relay, then, the written text works according to a different code altogether, one that Barthes calls "diegetic" (41). "Diegesis" refers to the narration or telling of events in a temporal sequence, and is normally distinguished from "mimesis," the reproduction or imitation of how things are. In the comic strip, the written text is typically stronger than the image, because diegesis—movement forward in a narrative—is more important to the overall presentation than mimesis—the attempt, in the drawing, to depict a situation. So too, in many films, the dialogue has a diegetic function, moving the plot forward: the dialogue does not simply provide information for the interpretation of the screen image, but often renders the fleeting image a weaker complement to the dialogue's attempts to move the story along.

As we will see, Barthes will later return to this idea of how different codes—here the iconic messages of the image and the diegetic relay of the text—work together, often with one code overwhelming others.

But Barthes turns next to the further discussion of the non-coded iconic message, which he calls the "literal message" or the "denoted image" (42). He reiterates that we cannot encounter the "literal image in a pure state" (42)— that is, connotation will always be present when we observe the photograph, and we cannot see it as pure and simple denotation, as he argued in "The Photographic Message." For that reason, one must talk about the denoted image not in terms of its substance but in terms of how it relates to the other types of message. The first observation Barthes makes is that the literal message exists as "a message by eviction" (42). This means that one imagines the literal message only by imagining what the image would be if all connotations were stripped from it. In this case, it would be "a plenitude of virtualities," the "absence of meaning full of all the meanings," or (and Barthes stresses this is not a contradiction) a "sufficient message," simple and straightforward (42). This may be confusing on two counts. First, if Barthes insists that we cannot access or perceive a simple literal image devoid of connotation, then such "eviction" of meaning must be impossible—how then can we speak of the literal message? We can speak of the literal message—the simple and straightforward depiction of things—because this idea of a simple and straightforward depiction of things is built into photographic technology, *even if we cannot actually perceive it*. It exists as a kind of optical illusion that we imagine must be there, even if we can never see the literal message. Let us return to the example of the panoramic photograph of the mountains with the highway and car, labeled "Switzerland": even if our understanding is focused on touristic connotations of Switzerland (mountain nation, nature, cleanliness, romanticism, etc.), we will imagine that the picture depicts a literal message—the existence of those mountains, that highway, that car. This sense of a simple underlying message, says Barthes, "can appear as a kind of Edenic state of the image," in which it is "cleared utopianically of its connotations" (42). This simple or "innocent" message, then, is in some sense our perception of a structure of the image—we must imagine that the scene exists in a simple and pure way, even if we will never see it as such. This explains the paradox that might give rise to a second objection—how can the literal message be both "full of all the meanings" *and* "sufficient" in the sense of being just a simple depiction? This theoretical Edenic state, says Barthes, is both at the same time. We imagine that, before our connotations of Switzerland are added to the image, that the mountains "simply" exist. But we also imagine that the simple image contains all the potential meanings we might give it. Put another way, we imagine that all of the connotations of the coded iconic message are already there in the Edenic image, waiting for us to develop them.

Barthes develops this argument further by discussing what is unique and unusual about photography. As in "The Photographic Message," he does this by comparing the photograph to the drawing. In the drawing, we know that connotative coding is always present. For one thing, drawing always involves rules and conventions—we know that there are different styles of drawing, and that drawings will vary so much that we cannot say that there is a single "essence" to drawing (43). What is more, drawing always makes a distinction "between the significant and the insignificant" (43): it does not capture everything that it tries to represent, but perhaps focuses on outlines, shadows, dominant elements, etc. As a result, the denotation of the drawing "is less pure than that of the photograph," because the drawing will always register a technical "style" (43). Finally, there are always deep connections between the style of the drawing and the thing being drawn. To put this another way, because drawing is something that one learns through "an apprenticeship" (by learning the rules), it always involves a fundamental continuity between its denotative work and its connotation—the two can never be separated (43).

The photograph represents an altogether different experience—one "truly unprecedented" in history. It signals an "anthropological revolution" (44), and should not be viewed as the latest new and improved form of image but as a "decisive mutation of informational economies" (45). As a form of signification, it provides a new relationship of "signifieds to signifiers"—that of simply "recording" (44). This is an argument that Barthes' earlier essay, "The Photographic Message," hinted at, but is here developed more fully. The photograph "establishes" the consciousness of the thing's *having-been-there* (44). This sense of the thing "having-been-there" amounts to a new combination of space and time—"spatial immediacy and temporal anteriority" (44). It is, on the one hand, a duplication of the *"here-now"*—the photograph records something that is in front of the camera at the moment of the capture of the image (44). This is the spatial immediacy—this thing is right here right now. But on the other hand, we also understand that the photograph was taken in the past—it records something that was *"there-then,"* or temporally anterior (44). The photograph thus combines those two moments: the "having-been-there" is the conjunction of the "here-now" of the photograph and the "there-then" of what the photograph records. The existential impact of the "having-been-there" explains why psychological tests rarely use photographs: the sense of something existing in the past overwhelms the individual's sense of self. This "new space-time category" (44) is what gives the photograph that message without a code.

What is most important about this "'flat' anthropological fact" of the "having-been-there" is that it "naturalizes" or "innocents" the connoted symbolic message. If I look at the Panzani ad, I will instantly register a range of its meanings as an advertisement. But instead of seeing this as a fiction, I will register the "literal message" of the photographed objects (net, pasta, cans, etc.) and feel that "nature seems spontaneously to produce the scene represented" (45). In fact, the literal message "disintellectualizes" the iconic message, making it difficult to analyze as a form of signification (45). This leads Barthes to conclude that the more photographs proliferate in the information age, the more "masked" the "constructed meaning" of the images will be (46). We may contrast this argument with that of *Mythologies*. Remember that Barthes said there that first-order images (like the black adolescent saluting) form an "alibi" for second-order mythologies. Here Barthes argues a more basic claim, that the photograph's depiction of reality (having-been-there) serves as an alibi for any connotative message.

We come, then, to the final section of the essay, which builds on the previous observations to outline the "rhetoric of the image." When Barthes talks about the image's "rhetoric," he uses the term in the classical sense: the tropes and techniques whereby the image conveys meaning. To outline this rhetoric, he returns once more to the problem of the iconic or symbolic message, which is full of discontinuous connotations. In "The Photographic Message," Barthes had argued that the connotations of the symbolic message are so strong and full that they overwhelm the denoted image. Here he develops a slightly different argument. Describing the Panzani ad, he had identified four connotative clusters (return from the market, Italy, culinary service, the still life). One could list additional clusters, but Barthes is interested in how these connotations work, since they do not necessarily complement one another. He answers that these clusters are not "anarchic" (46)—that is, we do not experience a chaos of unordered signification— but at the same time our sense of the connotation will be individuated. This happens because my own knowledge of the different sign systems at work in the image—Barthes calls these *"lexicons"*—will vary from another person's. The sum total of *my* connotative knowledge is my *"idiolect"* (47), and it follows that my psyche, my self, is the total of my understanding of connotative codes. Barthes spends some time talking about the difficulties of labeling and cataloguing these lexicons (47-48), but the larger point here is that the meaning of the image is "not merely the totality of utterances emitted" but "also the totality of utterances received" (47). In other words, to determine the meaning of the Panzani ad, we cannot assume that its meaning is a comprehensive list of all possible connotations, but rather that its meaning must be linked with the possible connotations available to the interpreter in her idiolect. This, however, cannot be our endpoint—we cannot simply say that the meaning of the Panzani ad is individualized, different with each person, for there is an order or regularity to the image. Where does this order, this "rhetoric of the image," come from?

In a final reframing of the problem, Barthes calls the various signifiers of the image its *"connotators"* (49). These connotators are abstract—like "Italianicity," which could refer to many things—if they are "deprived of context," but they will assume meaning when placed in a "syntagm." A syntagm is a sequence of linguistic units whose particular order (what we more commonly call *syntax*) gives those units meaning. If I have a number of signifiers—*child, that, fish, big, ate, this*—they acquire meaning from their syntagmatic organization, which might be *"this big child ate that fish"* or *"that big fish ate this child."* Syntagm is an unexpectedly important concept for the photographic image as well, because the connotators in question are "scattered" and could add up to any number of different meanings. But in fact the elements of the photograph *do* have a syntagm, "without which...the discourse would not be possible" (50). That syntagm is the denotative image, the lay-out of the photographic analogon. It is through this denotative syntagm that the connotative elements are given their structure, their rhetoric: "they are 'set' in a syntagm *which is not theirs and which is that of the denotation*" (50-51). *This* is how the denotative, literal message of the photograph serves as the "support" for, or naturalizes, the connotative, iconic message. What this means, finally, is that in the photographic image, there are two "structural functions" that are at odds with one other, or "polarized" (51). With the connotative elements, there is a condensation or intensification of meaning in "strong" signs, but these signs are "scattered"—in other words, connotation provides intense meaning, but almost no structure that renders that meaning comprehensible (51). Meanwhile, the denotative elements provide almost no meaning, but nonetheless provide the structure, the "syntagmatic 'flow,'" for connotative meaning to function (51).

As a final note, Barthes hypothetically suggests an extrapolation from his reading of the advertising photo: perhaps what is true here (that connotative and denotative elements are at odds with one another) is true for meaning more broadly. That is, perhaps "the world of total meaning is torn internally (structurally) between the system as culture and the syntagm as nature" (51). Perhaps there are two major realms that provide meaning—on the one hand, the realm of "story, diegesis, syntagm, and the intelligibility of a culture," and on the other "a few discontinuous symbols" (51). We should appreciate here the shift in Barthes' analysis. In "The Photographic Message," he interpreted the photograph through the paradigm of the Saussurean sign, and argued that the strong connotation of the signified overwhelmed and dominated the weaker denotation of the signifier. In "Rhetoric of the Image," he reverses course, first finding some signifying power in the signifier, although that signifying power comes not through content but through structure. What Barthes has announced, then, is a shift in his thinking away from the isolated sign to the problem of linear structures, the syntagm of the sentence, moving through time. Signification is more complicated, and requires thinking through the relationship between the parts of a more complex and dialectic system.

3. The Third Meaning

"The Photographic Message" argued for the impossibility of access to the real world through the analogic image of the photograph, asserting that connotative systems always overwhelm the denotative. "Rhetoric of the Image" changed that argument, stressing that connotative interpretation is a slightly messier project using the denotative image as both alibi and as a type of syntagmatic infrastructure: by this argument, the connotative dimensions of the image are parasitic on the denotative "has-been-there." Furthermore, analysis could not simply look at the sign, but had to look at larger structures to see how different elements of signification interacted. *Image-Music-Text*'s third essay on images, "The Third Meaning," builds on these earlier essays to a very different effect. Before turning to its argument, however, we should consider a few differences announced in the essay's subtitle, "Research notes on some Eisenstein stills." First, Barthes focuses on a well-known cinematic director, Sergei Mikhailovich Eisenstein (1898-1948, abbreviated SME by Barthes), best-known for his innovative work with montage in films like "Battleship Potemkin" (1925) and "Ivan the Terrible" (Part 1, 1944; Part 2, 1958). In fact, this essay first appeared, in 1970, in *Cahiers du Cinéma*, the most prominent, left avant-garde French journal of film studies. It may be worth noting that this shift to film was unusual for Barthes. In "Rhetoric of the Image," Barthes had distinguished what happens in photographs from the "more projective, more 'magical' fictional consciousness on which film by and large depends" (45). A year earlier, in an interview with *Cahiers du Cinéma*, Barthes had even suggested that film was "by nature, by technique, more or less reactionary." He continued:

I believe that the cinema finds it difficult to provide clear meaning and that, with things as they stand, it ought not to. The best films (to me) are those which best withhold meaning. To suspend meaning is an extremely difficult task requiring at the same time a very great technique and total intellectual loyalty. That means getting rid of all parasite meanings, which is extremely difficult.[2]

Film, he insisted, was messy in its signifying, and saturated with "parasite meanings"; at its best, film would pursue the means to "withhold" or "suspend meaning," rather than convey signification with clarity. While this is not exactly the argument of "The Third Meaning," which is not a manifesto about how to make films, we will see that the piece's argument takes up this problem of suspension. It does so in a very speculative manner, signaled by the subtitle "Research notes on some Eisenstein stills." "Research notes" suggests something not exactly an essay, something more experimental, and indeed, Barthes' writing became much more experimental through the 1960s and 70s. We may finally note that, though this essay focuses on a notable director and is published in a film studies journal,

---

2 Barthes, "On Film," 21, in *The Grain of the Voice: Interviews, 1962-1980.*

it focuses on stills—frames of the film frozen, in a sense, as photographs.

Barthes jumps right into his examination of a still from Eisenstein's "Ivan the Terrible"—two figures pour gold coins on czar Ivan's head. In this still, we can find "three levels of meaning" (52). The first level is "informational," and accounts for all that one can learn from setting, costumes, characters, and the action depicted. This "message," Barthes says abruptly, "will be of no further concern" (52). The second level, then, involves more interpretation. Barthes calls this level "symbolic," and takes as his illustration the central act of pouring gold coins. Barthes identifies four ways in which we might interpret this symbolism. First, *referentially*, we will think of the tradition to which the scene alludes, the monarchical baptism by gold: this was an actual practice or ritual referenced by Eisenstein. Second, we may think of this symbol *diegetically*, within the story and plot of "Ivan the Terrible," where the interpreter makes connections with other scenes of wealth, gold, ceremony, and so on. Third, we may associate this symbolism more broadly with the cinematic *producer*, Eisenstein, and how he presents similar symbols in his other films. And finally, we might examine this symbol *historically*, meaning that we would look at this symbol's deployment and valence more broadly in culture. For example, we might read this scene as one of economic and psychoanalytic exchange—the czar is symbolically granted certain kinds of powers through this ritual act, or assumes a greater sense and identity of authority as a result of the ritual (52). Taken together, we might say that the first type of analysis amounts to a simple "semiotics," while the second, more complex analysis of symbolism is a "neo-semiotics" focused not on the message but on how symbols work within broader interpretive traditions: referentially, or in actual practice; diegetically, or in the film itself; within the tradition of the producer, Eisenstein; and as a broader cultural symbol linked with others forms of meaning, like economics (53). This second level of semiotics, which in Barthes' four moments gradually moves outward, is focused on what we traditionally call "signification"—a term Barthes has used very regularly (52).

With this foundation, Barthes asks if there is an additional meaning in the image. There is—this is the "third meaning" of the title—and it is a meaning that Barthes will variously describe as "evident, erratic, obstinate" (53), or, later, "obtuse" (56). It is difficult to know what this third meaning is—Barthes is "unable to give it a name"—but he can "see clearly the traits" that make this sign possible. The reading that Barthes proceeds to give focuses on details that we might normally ignore—the nature of the courtiers' make-up, the "stupid" outline of the nose or the clearly traced eyebrows, the pale complexion of one, the flat hairstyle of the other, the hint of face powder in the application of costume and wig. Let us leave aside for a moment the importance (or seeming unimportance) of these details, and even our agreement or disagreement with Barthes about his perceptions: why is he focused on these details? These details together signal a "signifier" without a clear "signified," a signifier that "possesses a theoretical individuality" (53). Such details cannot be explained referentially—we cannot assume that some real life courtiers of Ivan had such features or make-up or wigs. Nor can they be explained as part of the staging of the scene—it's not likely that the two courtiers seem different. As a result we interrogate the image, searching for the meaning of the signifier. For "something in the two faces exceeds psychology, anecdote, [or] function" (54).

Barthes calls this kind of meaning "*signifiance*," and in a basic sense, this essay is an exploration of signifiance, what it is, how it works, and why it's important. Barthes says he borrows this term from Julia Kristeva, who began publishing about the concept in the late 1960s. Kristeva distinguished the term from "significance" with a "c," which term is roughly synonymous with "sense" or with "meaning" as a noun. By contrast, "signifiance" is meant to suggest a more open and dynamic process of signifying, or "meaning" as a verb. This is how Barthes uses the terms: the second or symbolic meaning, the "signification," is what we know about the still's symbolism, whereas the third meaning, or "signifiance," describes a process of moving toward or finding sense. Indeed, Barthes clarifies this distinction in the next page. Symbolic meaning is "intentional" (what Eisenstein "meant"), and refers to general shared lexicons. It is "closed" in the sense that it does not depend on any single interpreter; one can imagine this interpretation persisting whether or not any particular reader encounters that signified. Accordingly, this kind of meaning is called "obvious," in that it exists before me, and "seek[s] me out" (54). By contrast, signifiance refers to an "obtuse" meaning— something hard to register, "fleeting" and "elusive" (54). Barthes plays on the literal meaning of obtuse—"*blunted, rounded in form*"—in three ways. The obtuse meaning "cause[s] my reading to slip" because it is not sharp, clear, and angular. Like the obtuse angle opening beyond 90 degrees, it also "open[s] the field of meaning totally," to new inflections. And finally, playing on the vernacular use of the word to mean stupid, the obtuse meaning is also "outside culture, knowledge, and information" (55). In concluding this first survey of signifiance, Barthes also notes that "it is on the side of the carnival" (55). He refers here to the work of the Russian literary critic Mikhail Bakhtin, specifically his book *Rabelais and His World*, which was translated from Russian to French in 1970: Bakhtin linked the writings of Rabelais to a popular medieval culture he described as both open to multiple meanings and subversive of dominant culture. In this reference to signifiance "on the side of the carnival," Barthes anticipates an argument that will become clearer by the end of the essay, where he increasingly suggests a political approach associated with this new interpretation of meaning.

As usual, Barthes returns to his basic terms to elaborate, first expanding upon some points made about "the obvious meaning" (55). He discusses several examples of obvious meaning in the adjacent stills from Eisenstein's films—for instance, the four figures representing the ages of life (image II). What he wants to show here is how examples of obvious meaning are clear and emphatic, trying to control our interpretation. Thus the "clenched fist" of image IV is carefully presented—showing anger, but, because directed downward and turned inward, also showing "clandestinity" (55). As such, the fist not only connotes working class struggle but also the dynamics of revolution—the present anger, the careful waiting, the "patience" and "prudence" of controlling one's response for the moment (56). It is clear that this signifier is neither ambiguous nor "polysemous"— that is, it cannot be interpreted in multiple ways. We do not see this as a fascist fist (lifted high) or a hoodlum's fist (waving, visible), but as a specific kind of fist, carefully situated. These examples explain why Barthes has chosen

Eisenstein to explore signifiance: for "Eisensteinian meaning," so careful and emphatic, "devastates ambiguity," and therefore tries as much as possible to eliminate the variability of interpretations (56). So in image III, we have a "classic" expression of grief—women with bowed heads, faces indicative of suffering, hand covering a sob. But Eisenstein characteristically adds even more emphatic details—what Barthes calls his "decorativism"—to drive this interpretation home: the hands carefully arranged, and gestures and postures evoking Russian icons and the Christian *pietà* (56). These additional details "accentuate" the meaning of the Eisensteinian scene (56).

Barthes now returns to the obtuse or third meaning. His earlier examples—the stupid looking face, the uneven make-up, and so on—may make the third meaning seem like something idiosyncratic, something that I subjectively alone see, perhaps even something that I seem to project into the image. The discussion that follows is an attempt to move beyond this initial impression, and to clarify the stakes of the third meaning. Barthes begins by reconstructing his response to one of the presented stills, image V, which he contrasts to image VI. In both images we see the craft of the Eisensteinian image—the carefully staged facial expression, body language, and clothing. Barthes offers a reconstruction of his reaction to the first still—he sensed an obtuse meaning, struggled to locate it, and concluded that it had something to do with "the region of the forehead" (57). But when he looked at image VI, that obtuse meaning was not present, and it was at that moment that he "understood that the scandal, supplement or drift imposed on this classic representation of grief came very precisely from a tenuous relationship" of the headscarf, the eyes, and the "convex mouth" (57). What Barthes goes on to describe—and the difficulty of the description is part of the issue—are the elements of "a rather pitiful disguise" somewhat like that of "a facetious, simpleton look" (57). Put another way, what Barthes seems to see is the contrived and slightly overdone nature of the image, where Eisenstein has gone a bit too far in his accentuation—evident in the still where the old woman's eyes are closed, not evident in the second still where her eyes are open. Consider another example, found in image VII, where czar Ivan raises his head: here Barthes notes the "artifice" of the beard (58).

With either example, we might look at the still and see the obvious meaning, or we might see the obtuse meaning—the meaning intended by Eisenstein, or some sign of the artificiality or disguise of the scene. The result is a "dialogism" or "oscillation"—a back-and-forth communication between these two views, obvious and obtuse—in which one can capture the process of meaning taking shape (57). In the terms used earlier, we can see the moment of signification, but we can also see, in the third meaning, the process or "temporality" of meaning, its signifiance. It is not that we are debunking such scenes, by saying, here, look at this artificiality, this contrived construction of an image. What we are seeing, rather, is a "multi-layering of meanings" as in "a geological formation": we see the effective obvious meaning *and*, at the same time, signs of the attempt to construct that meaning (58). Barthes formulates this apparent paradox in a number of ways. Referring to the false beard of czar Ivan, he describes it as at once revealing "its fissure and its suture" (58). We see at once the fabricated nature of the beard (the "fissure" where the disguise is attached) *and* its effectiveness as a sign (the "suture" where the beard joins chin to signify imperial authority, arrogance, etc.). This is an important point, for Barthes is not suggesting that the "third meaning" opens up a "parodic" or "derisive" interpretation alone: it is not that the third meaning allows us to look at the still and say that it is false. The *derision* of expressions that reveal a "third meaning" are "*non-negating*," meaning that they do not cancel out their obvious reading.

The point with these examples is not to find where Eisenstein comes up short, but to develop a sense of Eisenstein's style, something Barthes develops in the example of image IX, in which a proletarian woman addresses workers, her hand raised in a (relatively) small fist. Here Barthes locates a third meaning in the woman's hair bun. The bun does not add to the meaning of the image, but "gives the woman something *touching*...or *sensitive*" (58-59). Such an observation may seem inappropriately vague and subjective, and one can hardly imagine Barthes using such terms in the preceding essays, but he wants to defend this kind of terminology, however "antiquated" it may seem. What he is trying to describe, after all, is a kind of feeling evoked by the image—"a certain *emotion*"—that in this case "simply *designates* what one loves, what one wants to defend" (59). Barthes quickly adds that this emotional response is actually evoked frequently in Eisenstein's work, which "is constantly informed by something loving": one might even say that "the Eisensteinian people is essentially *lovable*" (59). One might say that our reaction is erotic—not in an overtly sexual way, but insofar as we are sensually moved in some way by what we see. This eroticism may also include "the contrary of the beautiful, as also what falls outside such contrariety"—for example, the ugliness of the Euphrosyne (Efrosinia) character of images XII and XIII, or the ridiculously flabby and soft sense of the children in image XV. The point here is not the positive portrayal, but that there is a characteristic to the portrayal (lovability, ugliness, softness) that at once defies clear designation as signification, while at the same time revealing something about the process of signifiance. Consequently, Barthes can begin to characterize Eisensteinian obtuse meaning—there is something about how Eisenstein frequently presents his characters that can be captured with the third meaning. One might therefore use the third meaning to identify some tendency in certain "*authors* of films" or "in a certain manner of reading 'life' and so 'reality' itself" (60). Here Barthes brings up the example of image XVI, a still from the Russian director Mikhail Romm's 1965 documentary "Ordinary Fascism," which compiled footage and photographs from fascist regimes. In the image in question, we see the prominent Nazi official Hermann Goering participating in an archery demonstration. Whatever significance we might find here (Nazi glorification of strength, weaponry, archaic practices, violence, etc.), we can also detect a third or obtuse meaning—for example in the stupid look of the quiver-bearer, in Goering's "trashy ring," in the "imbecile smile" of the "arse-licker" in the background, and so on (60). What we are seeing here is something that is not quite signification, something that expresses Mikhail Romm's way of looking at the world, of filming (or editing) it to produce meaning.

Barthes is aware that he is trying to develop a new concept not sanctioned by traditional linguistic or semiotic analysis. As he notes, the "obtuse meaning is not in the language-system" and does not readily appear in "language use." It cannot be "situated structurally"—that is, we cannot find it in any precise location—and "a semantologist would not agree as to its objective existence" according to the rules of analysis (60). Put another way, it has no clear signified, and in fact designates "a signifier without a signified" (61). It is precisely because there is no clear signified, because this signifier does "not copy anything" or "represent anything" that it is hard to put the third meaning into words beyond a basic "approximation" (61). The third meaning is therefore definitionally something "outside (articulated) language" (61). Does this mean that the third meaning is purely personal, or, worse, that it may not exist? Barthes insists that, even if we cannot clearly name it or describe it, we can talk about it: "you can see this meaning," he says; "we do without language yet never cease to understand one another" (61).

What Barthes is moving toward, with such comments, is a new form of criticism. After all, the obtuse meaning is itself a "metalanguage (criticism)," albeit of a different kind (61). It takes as its task not the observation and cataloguing of meaning—what Barthes described as central to the process of interpreting photographs in the earlier essays. Rather, this new metalanguage tries to develop a different approach to the film. How so? For one thing, because this third meaning may vary from still to still, noting different elements, it is "discontinuous" and therefore "indifferent to the story," the narrative that the temporal movement of the film keeps pushing forward. The moments of signifiance display a certain "im-pertinence of the signifier," he argues with a play on words: the signifier is now impertinent in the sense of disrespecting significance and obvious meaning, but it is also simply not pertinent to the narrative signification of the film. Here Barthes approvingly quotes Eisenstein talking about artistic perception, noting for example that our sense of "colour begins where it no longer corresponds to natural colour" (62). Just as color becomes important when the expected or obvious correspondence breaks down, the signifier becomes increasingly important in Barthes' theory of interpretation. One might say that the signifier associated with the third meaning is in "a permanent state of depletion," meaning that it cannot be decisively filled by an obvious meaning (62). But at the same time, one might say that the signifier "maintains a state of perpetual erethism" (62), that is, an unusual state of extreme irritability or sensitivity. The metaphor here is intended to suggest something like an itch that constantly evokes a response (scratching, rubbing, pressing, attention), to be contrasted to the "spasm of the signified" in which one instantly and decisively determines the signification, only to return "back into the peace of nominations" (62). This is to suggest that a criticism based on the third meaning might never settle on the task of clear description and delineation, but would instead seek out the *"accent"* or "fold" of signifiance. The former metaphor, the accent, suggests that one is not looking for the letter of meaning, but a particular inflection (like the accent on the letter é); the latter metaphor suggests a "crease," a point where meaning is so bunched up or crinkled as to become messy and productive—a "heavy layer of information and significations" (62). Barthes even appeals to Japanese *haiku* here, a poetic form that he repeatedly addressed in other writings of this time. Barthes believed that *haiku*, unlike western poetry, was not concerned with producing a deep meaning, but was rather concerned with the open arrangement of signifiers, to evoke responses rather than detailed interpretations. Here he offers a *haiku* about image V, suggesting that criticism's task should not be explanation (this is what the image means) but rather a kind of repetitive formulation, or what he calls the "anaphoric gesture" (an arrangement of details that generates a similar response) (62). The critic, in short, should not be trying to put an end to the process of interpretation, but rather should open up questions of interpretation just as the third meaning does.

As we have seen, Barthes' earlier essays on the image described how interpretation happens almost as if describing how a machine works: if he at times acknowledged variations, he in general described a structural process to which all interpreters were subject. But here Barthes has done something different—he is talking about an alternative reading practice viewers *should* follow. This is a prescriptive, as much as a descriptive, study of a "new—rare—practice affirmed against a majority practice" (62). The remainder of this essay, then, tries to consolidate this new reading practice in three ways: by clarifying a theory of *the filmic*, then by presenting a full-fledged theory of the *still*, and finally by hinting at a broader theory of the *fragment* applicable to other art forms.

Barthes approaches the problem of the filmic by considering a reading practice focused on the third meaning: imagine viewing Eisenstein's film, focusing not on the unfolding of the plot across time but on the "black veil" of one character (63). The result would be "a different film," one that breaks away from the proper narrative flow, even undermining the idea of character, which would come to be seen as "a simple nub of facets" or markers (63). In this way, we would be able to "subvert" the narrative, rather than destroy it (64). The narrative flow of the film works on viewers as a "strong system," but, if we focus on obtuse meanings, it is also a "stage" on which obtuse details suggest a very different construction of meaning (64). This alternative may appear to be "a mere parasite" on the full movie, something that "*slips away from the inside*" (64). It is with this alternative reading, however, that we can finally locate the "filmic," which Barthes defines as "that in the film which cannot be described, the representation which cannot be represented" (64). Our traditional summaries of the *narratives* of Eisenstein will be no different than what we would say about "a written text" (64). Only when we focus on the third meaning can we begin to approach what is unique about *film*. Put another way, only when we focus on signifiance in a film can we truly appreciate what makes film film rather than any other sort of narrative. Only then do we begin to approximate the complexity of our response to cinema.

The paradox of the filmic, then, is that it is hard to perceive when one is absorbed in the temporal experience of watching a film. When "in movement," one is caught up in the fiction of the film, its narrative moment, unable to see its components. For that reason, the proper study of the filmic must be grounded, at least partially, in the "still." Stills, Barthes notes, are often viewed as the naive or childish "subproduct[s]" of the more complex film: they seem akin to the pictures we fantasize over in shopping catalogues, a poor substitute for the real thing (66). But stills in fact belong to a different analytic tradition that might include the comic strip, stained glass windows, or pictograms (66n1). What the still allows is a movement "inside" the film, where the dynamics of a particular moment become clearer (67). One might think of the still, then, as a type of "quotation"—not a sample that captures elements typical of the film, but a "trace of a superior *distribution* of traits" (67). This last formulation is important: what we see in the still is how filmic elements might be *distributed* in the film at large, and it is with this sense of distribution, very much related to the signifier's dynamic of signifiance, that we can begin to detect the more interesting workings of film.

As such, the still offers us an example of the linguistic "fragment" (67). Instead of focusing on the misleading whole and its overwhelming dynamic—a constant problem in Barthes' earlier essays on photography—the fragmentary analysis allows us to shift attention to the more local dynamics of meaning. Instead of a reading focused on "logico-temporal order," we can begin a reading "that is at once instantaneous and vertical" (67-68), focused on the interplay of elements at a given moment. What the fragment allows, then, is "a veritable mutation of reading and its object...which is a crucial problem of our time" (68). If this idea remains unclear—a closing project that should be extended to other media—imagine an exercise in which you interpret a novel, a play, or a piece of music. If you approach the work as a whole, you are unwittingly privileging the horizontal dynamics of the work and the overall impression it leaves: you are focusing on one aspect of meaning at the expense of others. If you can isolate a fragment, however, you can shift your perspective to the more interesting and important dynamics of how meaning works across the work in question. Every other essay in this collection follows this program, in attempting some version of a fragmentary reading, whether in theater, narrative, music, or speech. It is this shift to the fragment that Barthes will explore from this point on, gradually shifting in his own writing to a fragmentary style.

4. Diderot, Brecht, Eisenstein

"The Third Meaning," as we have seen, moved beyond a description of how the photograph works, or how we read photographs, to a discussion of an alternative reading method, a different form of criticism that could resist unifying tendencies in photographic stills or films. This new form of criticism would focus on the "filmic," a perception that could at once read the "horizontal" elements of cinema (its narrative, its movement through time, its attempt to unify meaning) with a competing "vertical" axis, focused on the perception of the production of meaning. The goal of such a criticism would be to shift our interpretation from the passive acceptance and identification of what is there, to a more active discovery and perception of how meaning is generated—in other words, from a reading practice focused on the obvious meaning to one exploring the third, obtuse meaning. "Diderot, Brecht, Eisenstein" continues this argument. Like "The Third Meaning," it assumes competing interpretive practices, and seeks to locate more active and productive ways of interpreting: as such, it is something of a manifesto for how to read. But where "The Third Meaning" focused on a theory of the "filmic," in which the photographic still was contrasted with the running film, this essay, published three years later, tries to outline a broader artistic tradition (or at least an alternative tradition) that includes painting, theater, and film, while hinting at other artistic media as well. In fact, lurking in the background of this essay are music and literature, which Barthes identifies as different types of art.

To sketch the contours of this counter-tradition, Barthes focuses on three author figures, while mentioning several others (like the painter Jean-Baptiste Greuze). Denis Diderot (1713-1784) was a prominent French writer and philosopher of the Enlightenment. He wrote on a wide range of subjects (science, math, art, religion, etc.), often using dramatic formats like the dialogue. As Barthes later notes, Diderot expressed the interests of the ascending class of the eighteenth century, the capitalist bourgeoisie. Bertolt Brecht (1898-1956) was a German communist playwright, most influential and active from the 1920s through the late 1940s. Brecht wrote and produced numerous plays but has been most influential as a theorist of drama who challenged what he called "naturalist" theater of the late nineteenth and early twentieth centuries. Because of his own deep interest (and involvement) in theater, Barthes wrote extensively about Brecht throughout his career, especially in his writings of the 1950s and 60s. Sergei Eisenstein, as we have seen, was a prominent film director in the Soviet Union, and an innovator with montage techniques. Like Brecht, he also represented the "ascending" class of his time, the working class. What allows Barthes to group these three figures together as a "tripartite conjuncture" (78)? At the end of the essay, Barthes notes that Brecht, vaguely interested in Diderot as a figure uniting "pleasure and instruction" in theater, had once planned to start a Diderot Society for "pooling theatrical experiments and studies" (78). Among those he considered inviting to join this society was Eisenstein—hence the "contingent" juxtaposition of these three artists. But it is worth considering, as well, that

Diderot worked in or theorized a number of art forms—theater, painting, prose—while Eisenstein's work in cinema was inspired by montage. Taken together, the constellation of Diderot, Brecht, and Eisenstein allows Barthes to present a tradition grounded in theater but extending into other artistic media.

It will also help to acknowledge, at the outset, the difficulties in reading this essay, which moves slowly and sometimes erratically through examples of the works and writings of Diderot, Brecht, and Eisenstein to develop its argument. If this style seems frustrating, it is nonetheless an illustration of the very point Barthes is trying to make. For Barthes is trying to celebrate a certain type of theatrical, compositional art, in which the interpreter does not simply settle on a quick meaning or a sense of the work's topic, but rather explores a series of gestures within the composition. Our task, reading Barthes' essay, is very similar: we will not encounter a clear thesis followed by explication and argument, but rather must move through his examples to see details, here and there, of the work of Diderot, Brecht, and Eisenstein, arranged together in a tableau. To understand the essay, then, we need to identify the various interventions Barthes makes throughout, then think about the overall composition and how these interventions might fit together or interact with one another.

Barthes begins the essay with a rather cryptic thought experiment. "Let us imagine," he says, that ancient Greek culture established the importance of two interlinked disciplines, "mathematics and acoustics" (69). We should realize, Barthes immediately adds, that this historic linkage has been "somewhat repressed" by a different pairing: "the relationship between geometry and theatre" (69). We will return to this fleeting reference to mathematics and acoustics later, but the pairing of geometry and theater is important because together they make theater a "practice which calculates the place of things *as they are observed*" (69). This is a good definition, for Barthes, of "*representation*" (69). We must appreciate, at the outset, the first of Barthes' attempts to challenge our common sense about art. We may normally assume that representation means that art tries to depict or imitate—to re-present—reality. That is, we think of representation as a relationship between the artwork and reality. But "[r]epresentation is not defined directly by imitation," Barthes insists (69). What the Greek tradition understood was the *geometrical* dimension of theater—that it is not about *how things really are* but rather about "the place of things *as they are observed.*" What happens on the stage only has meaning if it is seen by the spectator. Thus "[t]he stage is the line which stands across the path of the optic pencil" (69). We might think of a geometric shape that is roughly a triangle. At one point is the eye of the spectator; two of the sides of the triangle extend to the two sides of the stage, left and right, designating one's field of vision; the third side of the triangle is the line cut by the arrangement of objects on the stage. Representation therefore always involves a subject (the spectator) "cast[ing] his *gaze* towards a horizon on which he cuts out the base of a triangle, his eye (or his mind) forming the apex" (69). A useful "Organon" or model of representation will always combine "the sovereignty of the act of cutting out [*découpage*] and the unity of the subject of that action" (69-70). In other words, the best analysis of representation will examine the isolation of visible elements—what is visible on the stage—in relation to the unifying arrangement of those elements. Barthes quickly adds that the "substance of the various arts will therefore be of little importance": it matters little if we are talking about theater or cinema (the clearest illustrations of this geometric framework), or if we are talking about painting, photography, or even traditional literary discourse, for they can all be understood as representational in this geometric way. All of these artistic forms are representational not because they imitate reality but because they are "*dioptric arts*," defined by how spectators engage them from a specific distance.

Here Barthes turns to Diderot, who, in arguing that theater is best understood as a series of tableau paintings, similarly appreciated the geometrical aspect of theater. Diderot in fact understood an effective play as a "gallery" or "exhibition" of sorts, of carefully crafted scenes like paintings (70). What he was suggesting was that the artist (the playwright, like the painter) should carefully arrange elements not to suit the unfolding of events or dialogue, but as a visual scene. The scene is "*laid out*" in much the same way that the "*table is laid*"—that is, with a careful attention to the spatial arrangement of elements (71). This artistic care— "demiurgic discrimination"—implies that the theatrical tableau is "intellectual" in two different senses: "it has something to say (something moral, social) but it also says that it knows how this must be done" (70). That is, it has a claim to make, but it also presents insights into *how that claim is made*. This is what Barthes means when he says the essay is both "significant and propaedeutical"—it has a clear (one might say "obvious") meaning or signification, but it also provides basic instruction in how to understand the tableau (70). It is both "impressive"—impressing a meaning on the spectator—"and reflexive"—reflecting on how that meaning is constructed; it is both "moving and conscious of the channels of emotion" (70). We might think there of Barthes' description of the third meaning and how it related to the obvious meaning; Barthes says that if one is attuned to the third meaning, one's perceptions will oscillate back and forth between the obvious meaning of the still (its signification) and how the still attempts to present meaning (its signifiance). The theatrical tableau is very similar, in that it invites two different perceptions, one accepting the tableau as truth ("something to say"), the other attuned to how the tableau is arranged ("how this must be done").

But Barthes' point is not simply that there are two dimensions to the tableau, for he wants to stress the confusion that may result from these two inflections. For the tableau (theatrical or otherwise) may become a "fetish-object" (71). A fetish is an object to which we ascribe powers or qualities that actually belong to broader human activity, or, to think of a sexual fetish, a body part or object to which we attribute an erotic power in place of the person or the full body. For example, we may treat a lucky charm (like a rabbit's foot) as a fetish if we think it has the power to determine the outcome of some event, when in fact, it is human activity that will determine that outcome. If we look at the theatrical tableau, and see only its "ideal meaning" or significance, we have turned the tableau into a fetish object: we believe it is true not because of how someone arranged the scene, but because the scene is there. If we see a play and think it represents some form of truth—"Good, Progress, the Cause, the triumph of the just History"—we have turned the play into a fetish-object, and have fallen back into the naive sense of representation, assuming incorrectly that the dramatic scene is presenting things as they actually are. We can resist this fetishizing process if we remain focused on the other dimension of the tableau—its composition. If we observe the theatrical scene noting how it is assembled, aware that this arrangement is attempting to create meaning, then we understand the more active meaning of representation, as the arrangement of elements for a spectator. How did Diderot understand this distinction? Barthes quotes one of Diderot's essays in which he describes the response of the spectator to such a tableau: the spectator either sees the elements at work so effectively that they seem like "the members of the body of an animal," or so scattered that they seem like random depictions of body parts (71). Barthes reads this observation as an insight into the "dialectic of desire": the interpreter wants to see the elements coordinated and skillfully assembled, in order to there see something as complete as a human figure. This figure then "receives the full fetishistic load and becomes the sublime substitute of meaning: it is this meaning that is fetishized" (72). Thus every effective tableau embodies a certain paradox. To work effectively to convey its message (signification) *and* to reveal how meaning works (signifiance), the tableau must be so carefully arranged as to evoke a tendency, in the viewer, to turn it into a fetish! In other words, the same care that goes into making a critically savvy, reflexive tableau also tends to dupe the viewer into reading the scene fetishistically. And indeed, Diderot, in describing how to construct a tableau carefully, encourages the artist to produce just such a fetish. He simultaneously provides a useful model of how to read art *and* encourages the misreading of that art.

In this discussion of Diderot, Barthes mentions Brecht and Eisenstein in passing. Brecht's appreciation of the narrow or limited Italian stage, and his hostility toward "indefinite theatres" (like "open air" or "theatre in the round") show that he agrees with Diderot's sense of the play as a tableau. Eisenstein, too, adopts this approach in his careful construction of scenes (70-71), and his films may be said to amount to an "anthological" cinema—collecting scenes in an anthology (72). In fact, one can imagine fetishistic viewers of Eisenstein stealing segments of film, hoarding them like "a lock of hair, a glove or an item of women's underwear" (72). For the remainder of the essay, however, the focus generally falls on Brecht and Eisenstein and the insights they share about the pregnant moment, the social gest, and the subject matter of the artwork.

We begin with the "pregnant moment," which is well illustrated in the sequence of scenes in an Eisenstein film. One of Eisenstein's great innovations is that *"no image is boring"* (72). No scene is inserted simply for background information or character development, and no scene requires that we "wait for the next in order to understand and be delighted" (72). Instead, each scene is carefully constructed around a potential event in the process of unfolding. Diderot theorized this as well, arguing that every dramatic scene had to be carefully chosen, "assuring it in advance of the greatest possible yield of meaning and pleasure" (73). Using a term taken from Gotthold Lessing's 1766 essay "Laocoön," Barthes calls this the *"pregnant moment"* (73), the moment which does not simply signify a value or a truth, but which speaks to how meaning will unfold. In Brecht's play "Mother Courage," there is a scene where the title character "bites on the coin offered by the recruiting sergeant"; this scene is important not for showing Mother Courage's distrust of the military or her attitudes toward money, but because it shows "her past as tradeswoman and the future that awaits her—all her children dead in consequence of her money-making blindness" (73). In this fashion, the pregnant moment foregrounds the potential of the signifier. It is the "presence of all the absences," meanings that have yet to unfold. Related to this potential is the fact that the pregnant moment is not realistic—we recognize it, rather, as "artificial," as a kind of "hieroglyph in which can be read at a single glance…the present, the past and the future" (73). In some sense, it is an arrangement of elements carefully designed to keep on generating meaning, which means that we should view such a pregnant moment with an eye to how meaning is produced, not the simple moral or lesson of the scene.

Barthes then builds on this notion of the pregnant moment by discussing the "*social gest,*" a concept developed by Bertolt Brecht in his theoretical writings about theater. The gest is not a gesticulation in the sense we normally think (like a waving of hands or shrugging of shoulders), but is meant to convey a broader social attitude. Mother Courage's biting of the coin to test its authenticity is one example, because it indicates a broader attitude toward money, people, and commercial transactions (74). The "excessive flourish" of a bureaucrat signing official papers— an example from an Eisenstein film—is likewise "gestual," as it indicates an attitude toward power, bureaucratic practices, and writing (74). But we should also appreciate how the social gest works in relation to the work of art. The gest is not important because it is "realistic," and one should not criticize someone like Eisenstein because his films are overly aesthetic or formalistic instead of realistic. The gest can be effectively conveyed through aesthetic forms (for example, in films that are described as "mannered" or "stylized"). Remember that Barthes is very critical of the naive view of representation as the imitation of reality. Accordingly he is critical of certain acting styles that function at the expense of the social gest. For example, he is critical of what is commonly called "method-acting," whereby the actor tries to present the complexity of the character as if the character were real. When Marlon Brando (a famous example of this style of acting) adds certain "facial affectations" to his character portrayals, he contributes nothing to the depiction of the social gest; critics may rave that such details make his portrayal more "realistic," but if the gest is not clear, Brando is doing nothing more than creating a sense of reality that makes him seem like a great actor (75). If an actor cries, and the tears "refer simply to the state of feeling of the Downcast" or indicate "he knows how to act well" (74), the social gest is being neglected: the tears should speak to an attitude of frustration in relation to other people or particular situations. Accordingly, the social gest, far from seeming natural to the theater or film, should resist such simple significations. Brecht theorized the response to the social gest as one of "distanciation" (also sometimes translated as "alienation" or the "A-effect"), meaning that both viewer and actor should be able to achieve a certain distance from the gesture (75). The spectator should not identify with the gest in an unthinking way, but should have a critical or reflexive attitude about it, even if she endorses it. To put this another way, the actor is trying to communicate a kind of knowledge about social relations in history, not merely knowledge about the character or about acting. Thus the social gest, like the pregnant moment, implies a creative and dynamic response to the drama, one that sees how meaning works, rather than the passive sense that the drama depicts how things are.

The tableau, the pregnant moment, and the social gest do not speak to the *content* of the theater, but rather to its form—specifically how scenes and characters should be selected, created, and arranged. Barthes puts this in stark terms: the dramatic tableau "has a meaning, not a subject" (75). Diderot similarly argued that the important decision for the painter was not subject matter but rather the pregnant moment (76). In the same vein, one cannot criticize Eisenstein for his choice of subject matter (for example, that it is out of date, referring to past events that audiences may not understand). For the important decision he made was about "the critical demonstration of the gesture...in a text the social machination of which is clearly visible" (76). This phrasing is important, because if it seems like the stress on form instead of content ignores social politics, the reverse is actually the case: content reveals nothing about how society works, but a carefully presented form can reveal "social machination." Or take the example of problem films, with a clear "topic," like movies about drug use. If they only present their topic (drugs are a problem) or simple moralizing (drug use is self-destructive) without meaning-generating social gests or pregnant moments, such films are empty.

Barthes finally provides not a summing up of his argument, but a balance sheet for the tableau extending through theater, cinema, painting, and other art forms. If "The Third Meaning" sought to identify a new interpretive practice—the search for the loose signifier—this essay has explored what this might mean in more detail. The pregnant moment, the gest, the tableau—these are all indices of where and how obtuse signifiers might be found, and how artists should produce them. But Barthes has also stressed several significant pitfalls where we might tend to focus, even in the tableau, on static, closed signification. This is the case with the *fetishized* tableau, or the misleading focus on content. Consequently, Barthes concludes with a balance sheet of sorts, returning to the question of representation, which must always involve a vantage point. For artists like Diderot, Brecht, and Eisenstein, actively working to promote an historically ascending class (Diderot promoting the bourgeoisie, Brecht and Eisenstein the socialist movement), this perspective will always be "legal" in a loose sense (77). It will always require the perspective of particular values and interests—some kind of "Law"—that need to be initiated, developed, and consolidated (77). Put differently, every artist "in a period of ascendancy" will promote a metaphysics of set values. What this means, then, is that even the art of Diderot, Brecht, and Eisenstein is internally split, with some elements pressing an obvious, some an obtuse meaning— some promoting the open signifier, some the firm signified.

This contradiction leads Barthes to ask if it is possible that we might move beyond the geometrical, representational constraints of art to something still more free—"When are we to have music, the Text?" (77). Here we must think back to Barthes' opening comments. There is a Greek tradition, generally "repressed," that focused on mathematics and acoustics. What would art in this tradition look like? We should rather ask, what would art in this tradition *sound* like, since it would not be a representational art entailing a geometric perspective. Rather, it would be an acoustic art that might *hear* in different ways, in different combinations, depending on our location. Think of a band performance, and how one might focus one's hearing on different elements from different spots—now following the melody, now the percussion, now harmonic elements, now the voice. While the theatrical tableau, as Diderot suggested, practically invites a fetishistic viewing (we see the whole thing as a full body), "nothing permits us to locate the slightest tableau in the musical text" (70). It is this alternative that haunts this essay, popping up in parenthetical remarks every few paragraphs. At another point, for example, Barthes imagines a "post-Brechtian theatre and post-Eisensteinian cinema" that depict fragments capable of "holding in check...the metaphysical meaning of the work" (72). This further resistance to the unifying tendencies of the tableau might lead, finally, to a different "political meaning; or, at least, the carrying over of this meaning towards *another* politics" (72). What this new cultural politics, grounded in a different sense of reading resistant to metaphysics and static interpretation, might be will be the subject of other essays collected in *Image-Music-Text*.

5. Introduction to the Structural Analysis of Narrative

The first four essays of *Image-Music-Text* nicely encapsulate several trends in Barthes' career through the 1960s. First, there is a constant redefinition and expansion of the object of study, as in the move from the apparently simple form of the press photograph, to the more loaded advertising photograph, to the complexly situated filmic still, to, finally, the idea of the artistic tableau as a site of visual perspective. What this indicates is that Barthes' analysis increasingly attempts to redefine the object of study itself, moving from the common-sense view of the image in the starkest sense (the simple photograph of the world) to the image as a marker of our visual and interpretive perspective of any number of art forms. Second, we see a steady attempt to complicate interpretive models. What began as an attempt to read the photograph as a type of sign shifted to the view of the photograph as a dual system of connotative and syntagmatic elements, then turned to a view of the filmic as the split between the horizontal movement through time and the vertical stacking of signifying elements, before ending with a dynamic model of elements in the tableau. This shift to increasingly complex models means that Barthes is increasingly attuned to different trends and tendencies within the object of study—some parts direct our interpretation in some ways, other parts work against them. Following from this, we see an increasing shift in Barthes' rhetorical position from a descriptive account of how interpretation happens to a prescriptive account of how we should interpret. As Barthes' analytical models become more complex, he increasingly calls for reading practices that privilege and endorse some interpretive elements while resisting others.

"Introduction to the Structural Analysis of Narrative" is our first detailed example of Barthes' work on texts, and places us in the middle of these three transitions. We see here an attempt to expand the object of study, as when Barthes announces, in the very first paragraph, that narrative is not simply made up of written stories but is to be found "in every age, in every place, in every society," and ranges across "myth, legend, fable, tale, novella, epic, history, tragedy, drama, comedy, mime, painting…, stained glass windows, cinema, comics, news item, conversation" (79). If his discussion tends to stick to written texts, he is already thinking about narrative in a much broader sense. Written in 1966, again for the journal *Communications*, Barthes takes up narrative analysis asserting, at the outset, a complex model of multiple levels. Drawing on the framework of "Rhetoric of the Image" and "The Third Meaning," he will explore the interplay between horizontal and vertical axes of reading (87), in an effort to present the text as a complicated network. (During these years, Barthes begins to compare the text to a computer, the newest model of complexity at hand.) While the project here is still heavily descriptive, Barthes will conclude the essay with some thoughts on how narrative reveals a "process of becoming" that helps us understand the human self, thus hinting at the prescriptive tone of the manifestos that will follow.

It will also help to understand that much French criticism of the mid-1960s has a very scientistic tone: many critics working in the structuralist tradition believed that the study of culture was finally becoming scientific and systematic. Instead of describing what were perceived as vague impressions and seemingly subjective attitudes and opinions, critics of this moment were particularly concerned with developing objectively true projects along the model of the social sciences—thus names like "semiology," for instance. This essay was in fact important to the development of the systematic study of narrative in a movement that has come to be called "narratology," a term first used by Tzvetan Todorov, whose work is several times cited by Barthes. This attempt to present a scientific method is apparent throughout this essay, as when Barthes writes, in a footnote, that he has "been concerned in this introduction to impede research in progress as little as possible" (88). But we will notice this scientific tone most obviously in the careful, five-part structure of the essay and in the continual introduction of special terms. The following discussion will clarify these terms, but it is worth remembering that our focus should be on the overall project and its insights, and not the details of the terminology that Barthes himself largely left behind.

The essay opens with an acknowledgment that narratives, or stories, are universal and ubiquitous—they exist everywhere. This omnipresence might make some suspect that narrative is therefore "insignificant" (79), a loaded term for Barthes. If narrative is everywhere, he suggests, maybe we should ignore it, just as one might not talk about the existence of air when one talks about speech. Maybe significance occurs elsewhere, in the differences among narratives. Perhaps our proper task is to sort out and classify different kinds of stories, a project common to many literary histories. For example, we might talk about tragedies, comedies, epics, and so on, defining narratives not by what they have in common but by their different characteristics. But Barthes insists otherwise, saying that we should try to understand what this abstraction called narrative is. We should try, he says, to identify and develop a "common model" (80) for all narratives, a "common structure" from within which all variations are developed and enacted. Here he appeals to the project of structural linguistics, which approaches the infinite variety of utterances by describing the rules of the language "of which they are products and from which they can be generated" (80). Barthes mentions a number of structuralist projects, including Saussure's work on signs and the anthropologist Claude Lévi-Strauss's study of Native American myths, both of which sought the underlying structure of their subject matter in order to seek "an implicit system of units and rules" (81). It is also clear that we cannot examine all possible narratives and then consider what they have in common—this "inductive" model is simply impossible (81). Instead, we must approach the problem deductively, trying to figure out how narrative works from particular examples (81). Then we may perhaps put together a "hypothetical model of description," and from that "single descriptive tool," begin to look at the "historical, geographical and cultural diversity" of narratives (81).

How should we do this? We used to study narrative under the rubric of "Rhetoric," but most rhetorical analysis, Barthes claims, has gone "over to belle-lettres" where it became "divorced" from the realities of language (83). Unsurprisingly, then, Barthes suggests that "the structural analysis of narrative be given linguistics itself as founding model" (82). At present, however, linguistics studies aggregates of language only as large as the single sentence, beyond which it does not venture (82). So if we examine narrative from the perspective of structuralist linguistics, we must assume that narrative is "operating on a higher level than the language of the linguists" (83). More than that, Barthes assumes that "the most reasonable thing is to posit a homological relation between sentence and discourse insofar as it is likely that a similar formal organization orders all semiotic systems" (83). In other words, he assumes that, even though they are much larger, narratives—which he here also calls "discourse"—have essentially the same underlying structure, and are homologous. If we can identify the workings of a phrase or a sentence, we can also understand the kinds of dynamics that might apply to larger narratives; in fact, we may consider a story as a "long sentence" analyzable under the same framework (84). What we are thus trying to establish, says Barthes in language reminiscent of *Mythologies*, is a "second linguistics" (83), in which we should see literature as a "language of the very conditions of language" (85). We may note, skeptically or not, the huge leap Barthes has taken here, in assuming that different levels of signification are homologous. Nonetheless, this is the gambit that leads to the following analysis—that *"The Language of Narrative"* is the same language treated in structuralist linguistics, but on a different scale.

The next section of the essay then takes up the question of "Levels of meaning" (85). To understand how narratives are structured, we need to understand the "organization" of the narrative. Any narrative is not simply the sum total of its elements, nor do those elements function equally. We therefore need a descriptive model that can accurately locate the level at which narrative elements work. Taking the example of linguistic analysis, it is often the case that a "unit belonging to a particular level only takes on meaning if it can be integrated in a higher level" (86). The phoneme (or basic sound unit) "mu" may have no meaning on its own, but linked with the phoneme "vi" becomes part of the word "movie." And the word "movie" may have no clear meaning until analyzed at a different level, for example of the syntagm: in the phrase "movie night," it appears as an adjective. And so on. The point is that linguistic analysis always assumes different levels. The linguist Émile Benveniste argued that two relations are of particular importance for clarifying the problem of levels. A "distributional" relation is important for units on the same level, while an "integrational" relation describes how units are related on different levels

(86). Barthes returns to this distinction later, but here wants to stress the need to "distinguish several levels or instances of description and to place these instances within a hierarchical (integrationary) perspective" (86). Simply put, the challenge is to describe the correct units at different levels (the distributional relations) and then determine how they are linked together in a multi-layered model (the integrational relations). Again, Barthes runs through several examples taken from other structuralist projects (Todorov's work on narrative, Lévi-Strauss's work on myths), but his basic point is quite simple. We cannot look at a narrative and think only about how it unfolds in time, even if that is how we read narratives. This "horizontal" dimension of any narrative is always complemented by a "vertical axis" which indicates a hierarchy of operations (87). Here Barthes offers an allegory for the model he is describing, in Edgar Allan Poe's detective story "The Purloined Letter." In that story, the police commissioner is searching for a stolen letter, and undertakes a detailed search of a room in which he is sure the letter exists. He cannot find the letter, which is not hidden as one might expect. The detective Dupin manages to find the letter, which has been refolded, labeled with a different address, and placed on a mantelpiece where everyone can see it. Dupin was able to find the letter because he began to think about concealment on a different level. Barthes likens the police commissioner's search to a "horizontal" analysis, always operating on a single level; Dupin succeeds in finding the letter because he is able to shift, vertically, to a different kind of concealment (87). If we are to analyze narratives well, we need to be able to read at these different levels, not just the naive horizontal level of one unit after another. Barthes quickly and tentatively outlines "three levels of description" in narrative (88). These three levels are those of *"functions,"* *"actions,"* and *"narration"* (88).

We begin with the "functions," a confusing term, since Barthes uses it in two ways. Barthes declares that our "first task is to divide up narrative" into its "smallest narrative units" (88). These units will be called "functions," because they function to establish correlations within the narrative, to make it hang together (88). As a "term of a correlation," the "essence of a function" is "the seed that it sows in the narrative, planting an element that will come to fruition later" (89). "Is everything in a narrative," Barthes asks, "functional?" He answers with an emphatic yes: everything has some kind of meaning, for "what is noted is by definition notable" (89). Using a metaphor from information theory, Barthes argues that "art is without noise"—there is nothing that appears in a work of art that is simply sound that we cannot process or interpret (89). (In a footnote, he adds that this is what "separates art from 'life,'" in which there is often noise or "'fuzzy' or 'blurred' communication" [89n2].) Our challenge is to find out where—on which level or levels—that meaning occurs. Will these functional units correspond to the usual units of literary analysis, like "actions, scenes, paragraphs, dialogues, [or] interior monologues" (90)? Not necessarily, and in fact rarely. Likewise, they will not match up neatly with the psychological categories (like "feelings, intentions, motivations" and so on) often used when critics talk about narratives (90-91). Nor will they necessarily correspond to the units of "articulated language" (nouns, adjectives, figures of speech, and the like) (91).

Before exploring these functions in more detail, Barthes offers a few examples that might be helpful to consider.

His favored illustration is Ian Fleming's James Bond novel *Goldfinger* (1959). If we read a sentence that tells us "*Bond saw a man of about fifty,*" what do we learn? Our common-sense view is that we learn what the sentence tells us—that Bond sees a man and estimates his age. But this detail, in the context of the narrative, has at least two functions. First, it gives us some characterization of the man that may prove useful later on, in a "diffuse, delayed" manner (90). And second, it gives us some sense of the events about to unfold: because the statement indicates that Bond does not know the person, we can speculate that what will follow might be "initiation of a threat and the need to establish the man's identity" (90). Or take this example: "*Bond picked up one of the four receivers*" (91). Here the common-sense reading is again simple and straightforward—Bond answers the phone. But the word "four" in this sentence gives us much more information; it tells us that Bond is in an office that receives many calls (they need four phones), and that there is "a highly developed bureaucratic technology" (a bank of phones with four receivers) (91). The word "four" thus does not really denote simple number (how many phones were there?), but rather functions to provide additional information "beyond the level of denotation" (91). These initial examples provide some indication of how Barthes will approach the question of functions, and how they operate at different levels.

Barthes proceeds to spell out "Classes of units," and again, we should not get too bogged down in nomenclature—as he later insists, "the names are of little importance" (96). He wants to spell out the units in the smallest number of classes, and first asserts that we can group the functions into "two major classes": "distributional and integrational" (92).

Drawing on the terminology of Vladimir Propp, a Russian formalist literary critic, Barthes calls the distributional units "functions."[3] A distributional function is so called because it indicates a correlation of additional units on the same horizontal level, where they may be said to be "distributed." For example, "picking up the telephone has for correlate the moment when it will be put down," a later unit on the same level (92). Going to bed has as a correlate getting out of bed, sitting down has as a correlate standing up, losing one's breath has as a correlate regaining one's breath, and so on. We can further subdivide these distributional functions into two categories, based on their different levels of importance (93). Some of these distributional functions are important "hinge-points of the narrative"; Barthes calls these *cardinal functions (or nuclei)"* (93). These cardinal nuclei are more important because they signal the possibility of a forking in the narrative, choices that might take the narrative in different directions. They announce "an alternative that is of direct consequence for the subsequent development of the story," and as such they create, in readers, a sense of "uncertainty" (94). Other distributional functions may simply "'fill in' the narrative space" between the more important cardinal nuclei; Barthes calls these weaker distributional functions *"catalysers"* (93). These catalysers cluster around the cardinal nuclei and fill in the spaces between these nuclei, but without "modifying [their] alternative nature" (94). For

---

3   As noted before, this term has two uses—the specific designation of distributional units, and the umbrella designation of all possible units. But hereafter, Barthes uses the term "function" in the narrower sense.

this reason, they may be seen as "parasitic"—they depend on the cardinal nuclei (94). Do they do anything? Yes, they have a "purely chronological function" in moving the narrative forward. So, too, do the cardinal nuclei, which provide the main substance of the chronological narrative. But the cardinal nuclei are "consequential"—the narrative can move in different directions—*and* consecutive—they are presented in a sequence—whereas the catalysers are *only* consecutive. Catalysers do not change the course of events, but merely fill in the illusion of temporal movement.

Let us take an example of a distributed sequence: **the telephone rings**, *Bond moves swiftly towards the desk, Bond picks up the receiver, Bond puts down his cigarette, Bond clears his throat, he notes that it is three o'clock*, **Bond answers the phone**. In this sequence, *the telephone rings* is a cardinal function, because it can have many different outcomes: Bond may answer the phone, Bond may ignore the phone call, the phone may stop ringing before he answers, Bond may trace the call, and so on. The outcome is set with the last unit of the sequence, *Bond answers the phone*, which is also a cardinal function, because it again announces a range of possibilities that affect the direction of the narrative: Bond may not speak into the phone, Bond may identify himself, Bond may disguise himself, it may be a stranger, it may be an acquaintance, and so on. But between those two cardinal nuclei (in bold face above) we find a string of catalysers. These catalysers do not direct or disrupt the action. What Bond does with his cigarette doesn't matter; his movement closer to the phone does not need to be mentioned (in fact, the sequence could be written with him standing next to the phone). One could imagine a range of different catalysers that might fill out the same space between the cardinal nuclei (*Bond checked his watch, Bond turned to the left, Bond grimaced, Bond noted a thread on his sleeve*), and one could likewise imagine a narrative sequence without those catalysers (*the telephone rings, Bond answers the phone*).

There are several things that become clear from this analytical distinction. For one, we can see where the "'telescoping' of logic and temporality" take place—in the cardinal nuclei. It is the nuclei that provide the strongest contours of the plot, because they entail the greatest "risk," the points at which the plot sequence can go in different directions (94-95). This does not mean that they are spectacular or huge events—"the telephone rings" is neither—but only that they can change the narrative in fundamental ways (94-95). By contrast, the catalysers are weaker moments, moments of "safety, rests, luxuries" (95); they will not determine where the larger plot goes. That does not make them unimportant, however, for how catalysers are deployed will have several important consequences. As Barthes later notes, the expansion of catalysers is what creates a sense of suspense, drawing out the temporal sequence as the reader awaits the cardinal correlate (119). In a similar vein, the catalysers may play a special role in distracting or misleading. In a detective novel, the investigator's observations may constitute a long series of catalysers (*she saw a ticket stub in the corpse's hand, to her left she heard a cat screech, a taxi honked its horn, she smelled the faint scent of jasmine...*), and it may not be clear which of those catalysers is important, which merely feints to mislead the reader. In every case, the catalyser plays an important role in the "economy of the message," whether that means that "it accelerates, delays, gives fresh impetus to the discourse,...summarizes, anticipates, [or] sometimes even leads astray" (95). In other words, our sense of the speed, direction, clarity, or momentum of the nuclei of the narrative will often be determined by the catalysers.

These "safe" moments, even if they do not have great consequence for the primary sequence of cardinal nuclei, still play an important role in our perception of sequence. And here Barthes points out a conceptual danger intrinsic to the blending of cardinal nuclei and catalysers. For in encountering a temporal sequence, we are susceptible to the logical fallacy *"post hoc, ergo propter hoc"*—after this, therefore because of this (94). In other words, we will tend to read a sequence assuming that the catalysers logically follow from, lead to, and link cardinal nuclei. This is why we often encounter narratives as embodying a certain sense of "Destiny"; if they richly fill out the horizontal axis, events seem not only sequential or consecutive, but also consequential (*d* happened because of *c*, which happened because of *b*, which happened because of *a*...). This is no minor point. Remember that Barthes, in "Rhetoric of the Image," discussed the structuring power of the syntagm, and how it influenced our interpretive sorting of connotative elements. What he describes here is how we perceive the syntagm, here labeled the distributional, horizontal sequence; although the catalysers are not part of the strong *consequential* structure of the syntagm, they will appear to be, and thus will give the syntagm a greater sense of logical necessity.

Barthes mentions one other important function of the catalysers: they are "phatic," meaning they serve to establish basic interactive continuity between the narrative and the reader. In fact, this is ultimately the most constant function of the catalyser, which "maintains the contact between narrator and addressee" (95).

Let us turn, then, to the second major class of units, the "integrational," which Barthes calls *"indices"* (92). If the distributional functions explain how the sequence of narratives works along a horizontal axis, the integrational units provide a sense of cohesion throughout the narrative. Psychological indices will assemble to form our sense of character, other indices may assemble to form our sense of setting, others may assemble to form our sense of the overall mood or tone of events, and so on. With integrational indices, we are no longer following logical or temporal sequences, but shifting "to a higher level" (92). As Barthes notes, these indices are not "operational" like the events of the distributional functions; rather, they have a clear "signified" to which they add more substance. One may think of an index (the singular of *"indices"*) in a history book, which will list all the page numbers on which we may find discussion of, say, Robespierre. What this index shows, in part, is how our sense of Robespierre is gradually assembled from these different references. In this way, the indices "integrate" the narrative vertically, so it is more than simply a sequence of one damn thing after another.

Again, Barthes distinguishes between two different kinds of indices, *"indices* proper" (hereafter simply called "indices") and *"informants"* (96). An index constitutes, over the course of the narrative, "the character of a narrative agent, a feeling, an atmosphere...or a philosophy" (96). All of these—characters, feelings, atmospheres, settings—do not really exist in the horizontal sequence of nuclei and catalysers, which are basically events. These indices exist on a different level, and they achieve cohesion and meaning from this process of indexing. *Informants*, however, provide "pure data with immediate significance"—they help us locate the narrative in time and space, giving us our bearings with brute information. If indices "always have implicit signifieds" (referring to characters, settings, moods), the informants do not: they provide "ready-made knowledge" though of a weaker sort (96). Though informants may seem insignificant, and do not add to the more important indexical elements, they are nonetheless "realist operators" that "authenticate the reality of the referent" (96). One might say that they create a "reality effect" (a concept Barthes developed in another essay), because they seem "to embed fiction in the real world" (96). Take this sentence from the beginning of Virginia Woolf's *The Voyage Out*: "One afternoon in the beginning of October when the traffic was becoming brisk a tall man strode along the edge of the pavement with a lady on his arm."[4] Several of the elements of this sentence act as indices: brisk traffic, the early October afternoon, and pavement all contribute indexically to a sense of setting and tone. The character here (later given the name Mr. Ambrose) is also developed: he is tall, so perhaps imposing and confident, he does not walk alongside the woman as her equal, but has a woman on his arm, and so on. Amidst these indices, "the beginning of October" is the informant, providing information that gives a sense of the reality of the scene by situating it on the calendar.

Let us consider again the sequential example from earlier: *the telephone rings, Bond moves swiftly towards*

4 Virginia Woolf, *The Voyage Out* (New York: Oxford World's Classics, 1992), 3.

the desk, Bond picks up the receiver, Bond puts down his cigarette, Bond clears his throat, he notes that it is three o'clock, Bond answers the phone. If we bracket the nuclei and catalysers for a moment, we will see several indices and informants. Indexically, we learn several things about Bond (he moves swiftly, he smokes, he clears his throat, he watches the clock). The meaning of these details may be clear from earlier indices, or may become clearer with later indices. His smoking may indicate that he is casual and cosmopolitan, or it may indicate that he is nervous; likewise, his swift movement may indicate a decisive and energetic character, or it may indicate anxiety. We will only be able to interpret these indices as they are assembled. The sequence also includes several informants: Bond is in an office big enough that the phone is some distance away, and it is three o'clock. These details may not add much to the story, though they provide a sense of information, and contribute to the realism of the scene.

So Barthes has defined four major correlational units in narratives:

Distributional Functions (horizontal)	Integrational Indices (vertical)
• Cardinal nuclei • Catalysers	• Indices • Informants

The distributional functions move the narrative along temporally, while the integrational indices assemble details at a higher level. Specifically, the distributional units work syntagmatically, while the integrational units work paradigmatically. More simply, the distributional functions correspond to "doing," while the integrational indices correspond to "being" (93). Of the four, the nuclei are unique in being "governed by a logic," and "at once necessary and sufficient" (97). In the nuclei, we see the temporal core of the narrative. In relation to the nuclei, the other three units—catalysers, indices, and informants—are all "*expansions*," filling out the nuclei with "duplications, paddings, embeddings and so on" (97). Furthermore, when we encounter particular narratives, our varying sense of what they are often reflects different combinations of these elements. An adventure story or a folktale typically is heavy in functions, while a psychological novel focused on character will typically be heavy in indices (93). But it is important to remember that these units are not mutually exclusive. An element of a text "can at the same time belong to two different classes" (96). Drinking whiskey in an airport lounge, for example, may operate as a catalyser (for the cardinal nuclei of "*waiting*"), but it may also be an indice of atmosphere (the modern experience of the airport, relaxation, and so on) (96-97). "[U]nits can be mixed" (97).

But whatever clarity may come with the identification or description of these units, several questions remain. According to what rules—Barthes calls it a "grammar"—are these different units combined in a narrative? It is clear that informants and indices exist alongside one another, that catalysers and nuclei operate together, and that some of the cardinal nuclei are bound together as a sequence, as we have seen (97-98). But a question remains about how *all* the cardinal nuclei are strung together. If *the telephone rings* implies *Bond answers the phone*, there is no necessary link, in narrative logic, binding *the telephone rings* to *Bond plays cards* or *Bond finds a corpse*. We have yet to figure out how the overall narrative coheres in its temporal unfolding, as it plays out in time. To put this in the more technical terms Barthes has established, it is not clear why cardinal nuclei that lack a relationship of logical reciprocity (one event implying the other) fit together. The issue Barthes has identified here, then, is how the narrative's temporality, its existence in time, works, and this speaks to a larger conceptual problem. If one approaches the narrative as a structure to be analyzed, then where does time fit in? Does time exist alongside the narrative structure, or as part of it? Is time an optical illusion of sorts that is actually an expression of a structure? Is the sense of time the result of semiotic activity in the narrative?

Barthes' answer is that time is indeed an effect of narrative, a "chronological illusion" (99). As a result, the task of a structural analysis of narrative is to locate the mechanisms and units that make "chronological succession" appear in "an atemporal matrix structure" (98). To date, he says, there have been three different approaches to solving this problem. The first asserts that the temporal logic of narrative tries to express "the syntax of human behaviour" (99). Actual humans have to make choices, and pursue a certain kind of logic; narratives transfer this lived syntax into a different structure, focusing on moments when "characters...choose to act" (100). In other words, temporality is already logical in human behavior, and narrative tries to transfer that logic to a different medium. A second approach argues that temporality is simply a delivery vehicle for a deeper logic of basic oppositions. Narratives seek to express this logic by transferring such oppositions (wisdom and ignorance, for example) "along the line of the narrative" (100). By this view, temporality is not that important, but is a way to structure a system of thinking that is not ultimately temporal. The third approach "sets the analysis at the level of the 'actions' (that is to say, of the characters)" (100). This means that actions are not viewed as events, but as expressions of acting agents, which we call characters.[5]

Barthes argues that these three explanatory models "are not competitive but concurrent" (100), three possibly compatible ways of looking at the same problem. Yet none of these approaches is immediately adequate for a long complex narrative like a novel. The novel will contain a wide range of cardinal nuclei, including some that are small and insignificant (*Bond answers the phone, Bond drinks a martini*). We need, therefore, a framework that can "account for *all* the narrative units, for the smallest narrative segments" (101). For the overall narrative "necessitates an organization of relays" between these micro-units; it must bind them together in some way (101). We may clarify this situation by returning to the problem at hand: some cardinal nuclei are bound together by a certain logic (*the phone rings, Bond answers the phone*). These logically-connected nuclei—Barthes calls them "sequences"—can be recognized and labeled, and may be either minor (*having a drink, shaking hands*) or major (like *struggle* or *request*). Indeed, readers, having encountered these sequences in other narratives will recognize them as such: "[t]he narrative language...within us comprises from the start these essential headings" (102). We know, from our reading experience, that seduction will entail a closed sequence extending from encounter, through interaction

---

5 These three approaches are associated with the work of Claude Bremond; Claude Lévi-Strauss, Roman Jakobson, and Algirdas Greimas; and Tzvetan Todorov respectively.

and deception, to some kind of victory and conquest (sexual, political, psychological).

So how do we think about the connections between these discrete sequences? Barthes offers two solutions. The first response is one he calls "stemmatic" (103). He notes that often a closed sequence will actually *encompass* other closed sequences. For instance, "shaking hands" is a closed sequence of nuclei, but it may itself be part of a different, also closed sequence, "greeting." "Greeting" likewise may itself be part of another closed sequence, "Meeting," which itself may be part of another closed sequence "Request" (103). While this may seem obvious, we have to be clear about the implications of this argument. The point is not that "Request" is a "bigger" string of many nuclei that will necessarily include a smaller sequence like "Greeting" or, still smaller, "Shaking Hands." For one thing, "Request" does not necessarily contain or include "shaking hands"— we could easily imagine a "Request" sequence with different nuclei (a phone call, a hug, sending a messenger bird, etc.). But the more important point is that "Request" is a closed sequence, just as "Meeting" is a closed sequence, just as "Greeting" and "shaking hands" are closed sequences. "Request" is not a bigger, longer sequence that necessarily includes the subsets, but rather a closed sequence that, in some narratives, will incorporate other closed sequences. What this means is that, as a first step in thinking about how closed sequences fit together, we must shift to the model of a tree of different levels, as Barthes shows (103). It is worth noting that while this stemmatic model shows these sequences operating at different structural levels, these are not readily apparent to the reader, who "perceives a linear succession of terms" (103). Consequently, we can say, drawing a metaphor from music, that "[s]equences move in counterpoint" (103), the highest level branch of the narrative moving as a kind of melody, into which, at lower levels, other melodies are often blended. It is in this way that different sequences are "imbricated in one another"—they overlap, encompass, or are encompassed in ways that provide a sense of cohesion (103).

Still, an acknowledgment of the multi-leveled imbrication of sequences (upper-level sequences incorporating lower-level sequences) does not completely solve the problem. In Barthes' example, *Goldfinger*, there are three distinct segments of the narrative that have no overlap. We can likewise imagine complex novels that follow different characters, or novels that jump across time. How are the sequences linked in such narratives? Barthes answers that we must still look for another level of structural analysis, that of "Actions" (104). In *Goldfinger*, what links the different segments, at the very least, is the figure of James Bond. But from a structural point of view, what is this thing called James Bond, and how does it work?

The first section of the discussion of "Actions" is subtitled "Towards a structural status of characters" (104). Why is Barthes discussing actions, which seem to be related to plot, as a matter of characters, which seem to be something else altogether? He is here following one of the trends for understanding plot that he earlier identified—thinking about *events as elements of characters*. We understand this in a basic way when we encounter certain stock narratives. Sometimes, watching an action movie, we will recognize that a certain character (perhaps the hero's partner, good-natured and earnest) will inevitably be killed, after which the hero will seek vengeance. Or we may, in a police movie, see a series of bureaucratic superiors (the chief of police, the sergeant, the commissioner, and so on) as all variations of the same figure (the suspicious and scolding boss, who becomes an obstacle to the hero's efforts to seek justice). We may, in a romance, recognize certain characters as "complications"—temptations for the hero's pursuit of the primary love interest—and as such less developed than other characters. In all of these cases, we recognize that the characters in question are really not at all like people; they are not all fully developed, and are often not taken seriously as persons by the narrative. So while the common-sense view of characters is that they are modeled on people, we as frequently recognize that characters are often not at all like real persons, but rather elements of the plot.

This understanding has a long tradition, dating back to Aristotle, who argued that characters are "subsidiary to the notion of action," so much so that "there may be actions without 'characters,'...but not characters without an action" (104). Think, for example, of the "chorus" in early Greek tragedies: the chorus, often an unrealistic combination of multiple voices saying the same thing, importantly provides commentary and information, but is certainly not recognizable as a person. In this instance, the chorus *acts*—it informs, it assesses, it observes—and as such is something of an action without a character: we may say that the action (informing, evaluating, etc.) is primary, and the chorus a secondary vehicle for the action. Or think of certain *types* that appear in the character lists of plays from the sixteenth and seventeenth century: often a name will be accompanied by a label ("the noble father") or names will be clustered together according to their function ("Courtiers," who all give advice to the hero). Or consider certain traditional narrative forms, in which one encounters animal figures (the tortoise and the hare) or simplistic figures (Prince Charming): these are clearly not persons in any meaningful sense, but are rather functions that carry out certain actions (moving steadily in the case of the tortoise, moving erratically in the case of the hare, rescuing the princess in the case of Prince Charming). Our modern confusion about characters—specifically, our tendency to equate them with our sense of human persons—stems from a tradition that begins with the bourgeois novel, in which characters are increasingly created to approximate something that we recognize as persons.

Structuralists (partly because they examine so many traditional narratives) have been adamant about not equating characters with people. As we have seen, some even "went so far as to deny the character any narrative importance," or, more frequently, tried to classify characters according to some kind of typology (105). "Structural analysis, much concerned not to define characters in terms of psychological essences, has so far striven...to define a character not as a 'being' but as a 'participant'" (106). Barthes finds the analytical strategy of Vladimir Propp most persuasive, understanding characters not as persons but as agents of particular actions: thus characters might be called "actants" (105), and may be understood as umbrella terms for clusters of sequences. James Bond, by this view, is not a complex entity mirroring some real person, but rather a clustering of sequences (from, say, the minor *handshake* to the more prominent *defeat of enemy*). If we stand back a moment, we can see that this shift from narrative sequences to actions (clusterings of sequences associated with characters) helps us answer our pending question: what links sequences that otherwise have no connection? One answer is *character*, but not because characters are like people, but because, in a structuralist framework, we must define the *character*, or *actant*, "according to participation in a sphere of actions, these spheres being few in number, typical and classifiable" (107). In other words, the turn to the character has not located something else to insert *into* the sequence, but is rather a higher level of sorting out what unifies the narrative.

But Barthes notes one important objection to this framework. Characters-as-actants do not neatly unify sequences, because most sequences involve more than one actant (or agent, or character), and therefore more than one perspective. That is, a sequence often "comprises two perspectives, two names" (106). Take the example of *fraud*, a sequence from the perspective of the actant who commits fraud; from the perspective of the other necessary actant, the victim of fraud, we might label this sequence *Gullibility* (106). The presence of multiple actants within a sequence therefore means that we must complicate this framework still further, and in two ways. First we must begin to think about "rules of *derivation*," when we have to consider sequences in terms of changing relationships within a story (106). In other words, looking at characters' relationships helps us think about how some sequences may be derived from other sequences *based on character combinations*. In a similar vein, we must think about the "rules of *action*," which is essentially the reverse process: that is, we are "describing the transformation of the major relationships in the course of the story" (106). In sum, we have shifted from thinking about the relationships *between* sequences (the stemmatic approach of the previous section) to the higher level of actants, to think about different combinations.

How should we think about these combinations? In the short segment titled "The problem of the subject," Barthes suggests a strategy (107). He accepts the structuralist skepticism about character and the attempts to minimize and focus character analysis with attention to "replacements, confusions, duplications, [and] substitutions" (107). In outlining characters in a complex novel, for instance, we should not do so by listing all proper names or referenced "individuals," but by recognizing that multiple characters often perform (through substitution) the same function. But however streamlined this approach might be—he mentions here several critics' attempts to compile finite lists of character types—this approach becomes too complicated and fragmented once one factors in the "perspectives" mentioned a moment ago. "[W]hen the matrix" of possible actants "has a high classificational power...it fails adequately to account for the multiplicity of participations as soon as these are analysed in terms of perspectives," while the reverse is true as well: once one focuses on perspectives, "the system of characters remains too fragmented" (108). What is the solution to this conundrum? Barthes sketches out one possible solution, which would be to consider the actants along the model of grammar, specifically of grammatical persons: the first-person *I*, the second-person *you*, the third-person *s/he*, but also a grammatical tense that has existed in many languages, the dual-person *you and I* (108). If we think about narrative actants and their various interactions, we may find that these actantial positions often correspond to grammatical persons. Furthermore, thinking about the combinations of grammatical persons in sentences, or even games, may provide a sense of order to the overall structure of narratives. Think about a sentence like *I gave you the book to give to her*. Grammatically, the sentence maps out a relationship between *I* and *you* but also between *you* and *her*. We might imagine narratives having a similar organizing logic, in which the relay between action sequences is correlated not only to actants (*I, you, her*), but to a grammar that links these actants together. Barthes is tentative about this proposal, to be sure: "It will—perhaps—be the grammatical categories of the person (accessible in our pronouns) which will provide the key to the actantial level" (109). In some ways the argument is one of the least developed in the essay. But for the moment, this argument allows Barthes to move to yet another level, the final level in which characters-as-actants must find integration. That level is "Narration" (109).

Narration, the telling of the story, is ultimately the highest—meaning the most encompassing or coordinating—level of analysis for Barthes, and he begins with a few claims about how we must approach the phenomenon of narration from a structuralist perspective. Barthes asserts that, just as some narratives feature a basic exchange between a donor and a beneficiary, so too narration must be understood as an exchange between the narrative's donor and the narrative's recipient: "there can be no narrative without a narrator and a listener (or reader)" (109). So are we talking, in the case of *Goldfinger*, about the exchange between Ian Fleming (the author) and a particular reader? No. Although many literary critics, at least of Barthes' time, focused extensively on the author figure, this is a mistake, as such an emphasis does not distinguish between the author and the very different figure of the narrator within the story (110). Likewise, the study of narrative has paid little attention to the figure of the reader. But here Barthes seeks to clarify terms: what we are trying to analyze is not the relationship between a real-life reader and Ian Fleming but rather "the code by which narrator and reader are signified throughout the narrative itself" (110). The narration is not the product of an author that is then consumed by a reader; rather, the narrative itself creates the narrator figure *and* the figure of the reader, and maps out an exchange between them. We may understand at least half of this argument if we consider the first-person narrative, which establishes a particular type of narrator (with a certain kind of voice, certain ways of passing on information) quite explicitly. But these narrators always imply a certain kind of reader. For example, the phrase *"Leo was the owner of the joint"* does create a sense of the narrator (he speaks in a kind of slang, he knows Leo, etc.), but it also gives us information about the reader created within the narrative, for it is the reader who does not know that Leo owns the joint, whereas the narrator obviously does (110).

Let us return, though, to the narrator, the "donor of the narrative" (110). As he usually does, Barthes surveys different theoretical attempts to explain the donor figure. The first of these is the traditional view that an author, through various facets of his or her personality, creates the narration in some way: the narrative is "simply the expression of an *I* external to it," like Ian Fleming in the case of *Goldfinger* (110-11). The second view assumes that the narrator is some kind of all-knowing consciousness who masters all details of the story, as if from the perspective of God (111). And the third (associated with Henry James and Jean-Paul Sartre) asserts that the narrator should limit the narrative to what the characters internal to it can know (111). What these three views have in common is the confusion of the narrator (and characters) with real people. In fact, however, one cannot conflate people with these entities in a narrative: "[n]arrator and characters…are essentially 'paper beings,'" or effects of the narrative itself (111). One cannot and should not assume a continuity between people and what happens in narrative, and in fact the authorial process of writing, of engaging with language, does not in itself match a real historical person. In other words, it is not only the case that *"who speaks* (in the narrative) is not *who writes* (in real life)"—that is, the narrator is not the author—but also that *"who writes* is not *who is"*—the author is not equal to the person (111-12).

In discussing the dynamics of narration, Barthes makes essentially two important observations. The first is that narrative language exists in two different modes, "personal and apersonal" (112). These two modes may be associated with the grammatical persons mentioned earlier, "person (*I*) and non-person (*he*)," the former being transitive, or using language in a performative way, while the latter is descriptive (112, 114). In assessing whether narration is personal or impersonal, we cannot simply look at the grammatical person used in the narration itself (112). Consider this excerpt from the beginning of *Goldfinger*: "he saw a man in his fifties, still young-looking." This example, though using the impersonal "he," is in fact personal, as it narrates from the perspective of Bond; we could therefore rewrite the sentence in the first-person ("I, James Bond, saw a man in his fifties, still young-looking…") (112). Or take this excerpt, which seems "personal": "the tinkling of the ice against the glass appeared to give Bond a sudden inspiration" (112). The word "appeared" confirms, however, that this is impersonal narration, viewed from a distance. Rewritten in the first-person, it would make no sense: "the tinkling of the ice against the glass appears to give me,

James Bond, a sudden inspiration." Traditional narratives by and large adopt an impersonal mode, though in modern narrative, the "personal instance" has "gradually invaded narrative," focusing on the here and now "of the locutionary act" (112). As a result, most narration constantly moves back and forth between the personal and impersonal modes, as in the case of the sentence mapped by Barthes (113). Barthes discusses several examples of the mixing of these modes, and also comments on trends in narration—for instance, the avant-garde effort to shift to fully personal narration (114).

Why is this observation important? Here, as throughout the essay, Barthes wants to stress that narrative is a complex linguistic structure. Accordingly, he points out a number of confusions, traps, into which we fall when we read. Our confusion about the author and the narrator is directly related to the increased blending of personal and impersonal modes, which make it hard to appreciate that we are talking about dimensions of language and not an author's attitudes or behaviors. For that reason, it is important for Barthes to stress that "personal" narration—as in the "contemporary literature" he mentions—is *not* therefore more authorial or biographical. "Personal," remember, is a mode of narration stressing a perspective (that of the first-person I). As a result, narratives written more fully in the personal mode are not more "personal" in the biographical sense (that is, giving more of the attitudes or opinions of the author), but are rather more expressive of a dynamic of one language form (114).

This brings us to Barthes' second and related point, that of the "narrative situation" (114). What we must understand about narrative is that it follows a number of careful "codes" or "signs" (114). This is readily obvious when we look at older narrative works, like, say, *The Iliad*, which is historically related to oral traditions. We know that in oral literatures, and the written modes influenced by them, there are a number of very clear "codes of recitation," like "metrical formulae" and "conventional presentation protocols" (114). This is clear as well with traditional fairy tales, with their set openings (like "once upon a time") or conclusions ("... and they lived happily ever after"). These codes make clear that narration is not about transmitting the narrative, but rather "display[ing] it" (115). Put another way, these codes are not simply conventions added to narrative substance, as if the story could exist independently; rather, these codes permeate the entire narrative, and actually constitute it. The narrative "situation" is what explains our knowledge of these codes of narration. Someone from the fourteenth century would perhaps not understand a modern narrative, just as we sometimes struggle to understand narratives from different social and historical contexts. But we nonetheless have an extensive knowledge, accumulated from our long contact with narratives, that gives us an understanding of how to interpret the dimensions of narrative. This knowledge—"the set of protocols according to which the narrative is 'consumed'"—is one's narrative situation (116). This "situation" may or may not be conscious: we may recognize and reflect on certain conventions we encounter, or we may read them naively, through the misleading lens of common sense. Either way, the narrative situation determines the parameters of our interpretive abilities. No matter what narratives we encounter—"opening a novel or a newspaper" or "turning on the television," it is as if this act "install[s] in us, all at once and in its entirety, the narrative code we are going to need" (116-17).

With the narrative situation, we have finally reached the frontier of narrative proper—the point at which it ends and at which we can begin to talk about the social, historical, or psychological world outside of the narrative. The situation is the meeting point of narrative and world, and as such is also the moment at which we detect the "capping" of "the preceding levels" (117). The codes of narration, "install[ed]" in us (117), thus signal the terminus of a complex narrative model, that in this particular version has five layers. Most fundamentally, there exists a series of distributional functions divided into nuclei and catalysers; a higher analytical level of sequences; a still higher level of actants (characters); and a still higher level of narration. All of these are traversed by a vertical axis of integrational indices (divided into indices and informants), and analytically capped by the narrative situation. Such is the "System of Narrative" (117).

As Barthes himself argued, the terms and concepts of his model are tentative and open to revision, so it would not be helpful to treat his model as analogous to a schematic for electronics. Our task is not to plug every narrative into this model, but to consider what insights the model evokes, how it allows us to rethink narrative. There are four primary insights that may be summarized.

First, the structural analysis itself demands that we consider elements of narrative beyond our common-sense view. What we take to be plot must be considered from a different perspective (in terms of distributional functions, sequences, actants, and narration), which will allow us to move beyond a passive view of one event after another. What we take to be characters are not fictional counterparts to real people, but structures that importantly aggregate action sequences. Narration is not the speaking of the author, nor even the speaking of a fictional persona, but a careful interweaving of grammatical modes seeking to integrate actants. And so on—the point here is that we should consider how meaning unfolds, not assume that we are reading some straightforward account.

Second, structural analysis posits a complex interplay between different elements, such that the analysis of narrative can no longer read the entire system through an exaggerated emphasis on one or two dimensions. Barthes will follow up on this observation in some of the short manifestos included in *Image-Music-Text*, but here stresses how narrative "appears as a succession of tightly interlocking mediate and immediate elements," all with the complexity "of an organization profile chart, capable of integrating backwards and forwards movements" (122). Most bluntly, the narrative is a multidimensional meaning producer, an elaborate illusion generator with which we engage with remarkable facility, rarely appreciating the intricacies of how we interpret.

These first two insights, demonstrated throughout the essay, allow Barthes to conclude with a few observations about the *nature* of the narrative system. Language itself can be characterized "by the concurrence of two fundamental processes: articulation...and integration" (117). Simply put, the former "produces units" while the latter "gathers these units into units of a higher rank (this being *meaning*)" (117). Language thus generates signifiers and accords them meaning through different integrative processes: how the signifiers work depends on how they are assembled and ordered. Narrative demonstrates the same "dual process" (117). Within narrative, the production of units occurs in two primary ways: "that of distending its signs over the length of the story and that of inserting unforeseeable expansions into these distortions" (117). This "distending" or expansion of signs in narrative may be demonstrated by the example of James Bond ordering a whiskey while waiting for his flight. The whiskey will serve as an indice evoking several different signifieds (like "modernity, wealth, leisure") throughout the narrative; at the same time, the ordering of the drink may be a "functional unit" within larger sequences of "consumption, waiting, departure" and the like (118). The different readings we can give this short episode demonstrate how any "part of the narrative radiates in several directions at once" (118). We can find so many associations, connotations, and connections in such a scene not because we are "reading too much" into the scene, as some might complain; rather, we find that proliferation of meanings because that is how narrative works. In fact, suspense is not only a phenomenon of extended catalysers, as we noted earlier; the feeling of suspense that we encounter in a narrative—our sense that the scene is being distorted and extended, that the completion of the sequence is endangered by this delaying, is our sense of "a game with structure" (119). Perhaps the extreme form of this dynamic of suspense is the "shaggy dog joke," a joke that is deliberately and absurdly extended only to end without a punchline. The "joke" is how long the joke is, and how the suspense of waiting for the punchline provides the very dynamic of the joke itself: in Barthes' terms, we are experiencing the distending power of narrative.[6] The corollary of this expansive power of narrative is its integrational tendency. Narrative will anchor meaning through the basic logic of its sequences, the "strong and restricted code" of "the main actions" (123). It is important to stress this facet of narrative as well, because whatever meaning "radiates" from its distensive dimension makes sense because of this integration. Suspense is experienced not simply because of the extension of a narrative sequence, but because those elements are integrated to be experienced as suspenseful.

This claim about the essential qualities of narrative brings us to the essay's concluding observation, in which Barthes tries decisively to divorce our association of narrative with reality. Many of our misunderstandings about narrative result from our sense that they correspond to, imitate, or re-present an external reality: this is the source of our confusion about plots (seeing in them the logic of real-life events) or characters (confusing them with persons) or narrators (equating them with authors). This is the result of the shift to realism in literature, but such claims are "to be discounted" (123). To be more precise, the "reality" we see in narrative is not the reality of the world, but the reality of language itself. As Barthes puts it, "[t]he 'reality' of a sequence lies not in the 'natural' succession of the actions composing it but in the logic there exposed,

---

6 Barthes adds that this power to expand under the rubric of sequences is paradoxically the quality of narrative that allows us to summarize it or translate it from genre to genre (120). This is not the case with poetry, for instance, in which the language works differently.

risked and satisfied" (124). The "reality" of a plot is thus not based on its correspondence to actual lived events, but that it expresses a human "need to vary and transcend" the experience of "repetition" (124). If humans try to insert their experiences and knowledge into a narrative, it is not to reproduce it or mirror it, but because the narrative has "an emancipatory value" (124). Humans are in this case playing with the two competing tendencies of narrative—its distending, expanding trend, and its integrating trend—in order to experience, in a different medium, the interaction of freedom and constraint, what we might call the "process of becoming" (124). This interplay, in other words, allows us to experience all the passion that meaning itself, with "its emotions, its hopes, its dangers, its triumphs" (124). This is all that takes place in narrative: from a "referential" point of view, "*nothing*" happens, but in the realm of meaning we encounter "the adventure of language, the unceasing celebration of its coming" (124). This may explain why narrative is something in which children become interested around the age of three (124).

This concluding philosophical argument, celebrating narrative's manifestation of language's creative power of becoming, helps us to situate "Introduction to the Structural Analysis of Narrative" alongside the earlier essays on the image. There are some obvious similarities to "Rhetoric of the Image," in which Barthes argued that the advertising photograph generated multiple connotations ultimately constrained by the written textual anchor but more fundamentally by the syntagm of the photograph's lay-out. The argument here is similar, in looking at the freer play of signifiers regulated and controlled by the overall syntagm of the story—the core nuclei of its sequences. But here we have a full-blown theory of narrative as the conjunction of the two competing tendencies—the distending, generative power of narrative, and its constant integrative constraints. We are not quite to the argument of "The Third Meaning," where Barthes stressed the generative power of the signifier (signifiance) through the halting of the film and the selection of the still. The next essay will begin to move along this path, taking the structural analysis developed here as its starting point.

6. The Struggle with the Angel

This essay appeared five years after "Introduction to the Structural Analysis of Narratives," and one can see immediately that Barthes has abandoned some of the assumptions of that earlier work. While he partly declines to go over the rudiments "of the structural analysis of narrative" because it is "becoming well known," he also immediately asserts that such analysis is "not a science nor even a discipline" (126). Not only is he *not* describing a precise "method" of analysis, but he does not want to suggest "a 'scientific' view of the text that I do not hold" (127). In this case, he has chosen for text eleven verses from the Book of Genesis. He insists that the biblical origins of the passage—it is "a mythical narrative that may have entered writing (entered Scripture) via an oral tradition"—make it a perfect candidate for "an extremely classic and almost canonical" analysis (126). But here we must note Barthes' important gesture toward a *different* kind of analysis that he calls "textual" (126). Barthes the same year writes a manifesto for this "textual analysis," an essay, "From Work to Text," that we will examine later.

But here he gives some basic indications of what textual analysis might entail. It will seek not a comprehensive reading of how the narrative neatly works, nor of "how it is made" (127). He has no interest in historical criticism or a criticism devoted to illustrating the particular "difference" or "individuality" of the passage (126). What, then, is this textual analysis? It will show how the passage is comprised of a series of codes, "'woven'" together to create not "closure" but "an *open* network" (126). In a reference to the argument of "The Third Meaning," published just a year earlier, Barthes promises that textual analysis will examine the "signifiance" of the text, that is the ways in which signifiers become separated from clear signified (126). While Barthes had mostly focused on a theory of the "filmic," as the intersection of the still (of signifiance) and the moving cinema (of signification), he has here shifted to a broader meaning of signifiance in relation to the written text. And his imagery is bolder too: he says he will look at how the text is "unmade, how it explodes, disseminates—by what coded paths it *goes off*" almost like a chemical reaction. So while Barthes insists that he is not trying to stage a confrontation "between structural or textual analysis" and the "exegesis" of biblical scholars, this is precisely what he is doing here. He takes what is considered the most stable, the most interpretively rigid, kind of writing he can imagine, and attempts to "open" it up.

In short, this analysis will use a limited "structural analysis" as its starting point, and when Barthes turns to his first biblical passage, he quickly runs through the possibilities here for structural analysis. Structural analysis would typically examine this passage in one of three ways. It might, first, undertake an indicial analysis, specifically cataloguing how the narrative assembles "the 'psychological,' biographical, characterial and social attributes of the characters involved in the narrative" (127). Here, one might attempt to do this by tracking indices about Jacob (his strength, his attitudes, and so on) (128). One might also produce an inventory and catalogue of the characters as actants, looking at how they function to unify distributed sequences across the narrative. This would be difficult with our example, though, since it seems the passage "is essentially made up of seemingly contingent actions" (128), therefore perhaps *not* unified by actants. The third option for structural analysis would be a focus on the distributional, horizontal axis of strings of narrative sequences—"*sequential analysis*" (128). Barthes opts for this last approach *as a starting point, not an ending point*, and accordingly identifies three discrete sequences which he will explore one by one: "1. the Crossing, 2. the Struggle, 3. the Namings" (128).

Reviewing his reading of "the Crossing," let us recall the passage he analyzes, from Genesis 32:22-24:

> (22) And he [Jacob] rose up that night, and took his two wives, and his two women servants, and his eleven sons, and passed over the ford Jabbok. (23) And he took them, and sent them over the brook, and sent over that he had. (24). And Jacob was left alone; and there wrestled a man with him until the breaking of the day.

The first thing Barthes notes is that this sequence is repetitive, twice inaugurating an action sequence—first in the act of rising up (verse 22) and second in the gathering together of his people (verse 23). This kind of repetition is not unusual, but here serves to accentuate how the passage is internally torn, or dual. Barthes uses the term "strabismic," having to do with the vision of crossed eyes, to suggest that there are two perspectives built into the passage (128). One (located in verse 22) depicts Jacob crossing the Jabbok ford with his party; the other (located in verses 23 and 24) depicts Jacob "sen[ding]" that party. If one combines the redundancy or repetition of the two passages with this divergence in sequences, one has a text pulling in two different directions. To one side we have a "folkloric" interpretation of verses 23-24, whereby Jacob sends away his party to remain alone, to face a "trial of strength" common to mythical heroes (130). To the other (verse 22), we have Jacob crossing over with everyone. Now Barthes is not saying that the two passages contradict one another in some "factual" sense. One could read verse 23 ("And he took them, and sent them over…") as an indication that Jacob crossed over with everyone else, but becomes *grammatically* separated from them: in other words, he "took them" but also "sent them," and when all had crossed the Jabbok, Jacob was still "left alone" in a spiritual, if not a physical, sense.

How do we explain the split in this passage? It may be that we are detecting here the "tangled trace of two stories," as is common with narratives in Genesis. One story might be more archaically stylized, presenting the crossing as an ordeal; the other might simply recount the passage across the river (130). Barthes' important gesture, however, is neither to stress the contradiction (there are two completely separate meanings here) nor to resolve the contradiction clearly. As he says, he is not concerned with finding "some *true* interpretation" as is normally the case with biblical exegesis (130). Rather, he wants to identify "two different pressures of readability" that emerge from the overlapping of the two sequences (130). In other words, he is not locating two conflicting sequences (crossed or didn't cross) but two competing interpretations from overlapping sequences (remained alone physically, became alone spiritually). In the former reading, the mythic reading in which Jacob must face an ordeal to cross a boundary, the overall passage assumes a "structural finality": he remains alone to be tested, he is tested, he crosses over (130). In the latter reading, that structural finality is abandoned, replaced by a religious finality: Jacob, having crossed over, is now "*marked* with solitude" (130). What is more, our interpretation of this first sequence of "Crossing" will have an effect on how we read the other two sequences. If we assume the mythic reading (Jacob has not passed over, needs to face a test first), then the next two sequences (Struggle and Naming) will be incorporated into the Crossing Sequence. But if we assume the other reading (Jacob crosses over, and is then spiritually isolated), the Struggle and Naming sequences will be subsequent, not incorporated, sequences. Barthes maps this distinction in the stemmed chart on page 131.

We should appreciate how this reading disrupts Barthes' own project outlined in "Introduction to the Structuralist Analysis of Narratives." There Barthes had argued for the identification of distributional sequences of cardinal nuclei, insisting that such codes were integrated in our reading practices. The task, in "Structuralist Analysis," was to see how that sequence was then integrated with other dimensions of the complex text, for example through indices, through actants, through narration, and so on. What he is now arguing, however, is that the text is so split that this elaborate reading process is not clearly possible. While "there is sequential readability," there is also "cultural ambiguity" (131). This opposition, between an imposed, not really justified readability and a sense of ambiguity, finds expression in the different approaches of biblical scholars. The exegete, trying to analyze the intricacies of the text, might acknowledge the split, but the "theologian," seeking clear meaning, "would grieve at this indecision" (131). These two positions, as we will increasingly see, represent two competing attitudes toward the written narrative, the theologian stressing the effective and decisive structural analysis and clarity, and the exegete conceding that there is ambiguity. We see here that Barthes' earlier work is on the "theological" end of the spectrum, and that he is trying to use this structural analysis to pursue a very different reading strategy, one that "savours such *friction* between two intelligibilities" (131).

Barthes next turns to the sequence of *"The Struggle,"* focused on verses 24-29:

(24) And Jacob was left alone; and there wrestled a man with him until the breaking of the day. (25) And when he saw that he prevailed not against him, he touched the hollow of his thigh; and the hollow of Jacob's thigh was out of joint as he wrestled with him. (26) And he said, Let me go, for the day breaketh. And he said, I will not let thee go, except thou bless me. (27) And he said unto him, What is thy name? And he said, Jacob. (28) And he said, Thy name shall be called no more Jacob, but Israel: for as a prince hast thou power with God and with men, and hast prevailed. (29) And Jacob asked him, and said, Tell me, I pray thee, thy name. And he said, Wherefore is it thou dost ask after my name? And he blessed him there.

Reading the passage with an eye to its ending, the story is clear: Jacob wrestles the angel, holds him, and extracts a blessing whereby he is renamed Israel. But during the reading of the passage, we are repeatedly confused, struggling to distinguish one "he" from the other (as in verses 25 or 26). Is this because the syntax of the sentences is *"muddled"* (132)? Not really, for in the original Hebrew, the reading is probably clear. The confusion does not stem, then, from "an unpolished, archaizing style," as we might think, but rather comes from the paradoxical narrative itself (132). One need only compare the sequence with that "endoxical" (expected, traditional) narrative sequence (132). One would expect, in a struggle of A against B, that if A "resorts to some exceptional strategy," that A would then win the struggle. But here it is the reverse: the angel strikes a blow on Jacob, harming his thigh, but then the struggle continues on to sunrise and Jacob's surprise victory. Thus the expected narrative sequence (verses 24 and 25) is subverted, and shifts to the request for the blessing (verses 26-29) (133). Barthes plays with the conventional reading, noting that the "very god of narrative," of conventions, is defeated, even as the godly figure of the passage is defeated.

Barthes proceeds to connect this "complication...of readability" (131) with a larger trend in Genesis, whereby the standard order of primogeniture, the priority and privilege of the elder brother over the younger brother, is repeatedly disrupted. The most famous case of this, regarding Jacob, occurs in Genesis 27:36, where Jacob steals the birthright blessing from his elder brother Esau (134). The struggle with the angel repeats that structure, this time with God as "the substitute of the elder brother" (134). But Barthes is more interested in moving toward an understanding of the marking of Jacob in this scene. The sequence of marking typically requires a "situation of balance," after which a mark—of victory—is given (134). But here this convention, too, is disrupted. The mark is granted not because of a victory, but after the disruption of the sequence of a victory. It thus becomes a "counter-mark" (134), a mark against the conventions of marking. If we read the sequence, then, as a counter-marking, at the same time connecting this scene with other *Genesis* episodes in which the younger triumphs over the elder, we may identify the "function" of God in this scene. "[I]n this world God marks the young, acts against nature: his (structural) function is to constitute a *counter-marker*" (135).

Barthes introduced his analysis of this sequence by noting that "textual analysis is founded on *reading* rather than on the objective structure of the text" (131). He concludes by taking his structural analysis and moving toward a textual reading. Here, the sequence of the narrative (the archetypal struggle) is subverted in such a way that one's reading is confused, and in such a way that God emerges, at the end of the sequence, as the creator of a "counter-marker." What we see here, then, is a textual reading emerging from a counter-marking that itself hinges on a paradoxical diversion of the standard struggle narrative. In other words, the playing out of the sequence enacts a changing view toward language. God here "permits an anagogical [or allegorical] development of meaning," and "creates the formal operational conditions of a new 'language'" (135). God thus becomes the "founder of a language," in which one mark of the new language is Jacob/Israel (135). The confusion we earlier identified, reading the perplexing pronouns of the earlier verses, is not a syntactical confusion that could be fixed, but actually speaks to how the sequence is presented. And beyond the actual story—Jacob wrestles with the angel and is marked—we see here an allegory of how language and meaning can be created through the disruption of the conventional sequence.

Let us turn, then, to the last episode, the "*The Namings or Mutations*":

(27) And he said unto him, What is thy name? And he said, Jacob. (28) And he said, Thy name shall be called no more Jacob, but Israel: for as a prince hast thou power with God and with men, and hast prevailed. (29) And Jacob asked him, and said, Tell me, I pray thee, thy name. And he said, Wherefore is it thou dost ask after my name? And he blessed him there. (30) And Jacob called the name of the place Peniel: for I have seen God face to face, and my life is preserved. (31) And as he passed over Penuel the sun rose upon him, and he halted upon his thigh. (32) Therefore the children of Israel eat not of the sinew which shrank, which is upon the hollow of the thigh, unto this day: because he touched the hollow of Jacob's thigh in the sinew that shrank.

This sequence demonstrates a series of renamings, most obviously the reciprocal exchange between Jacob and God. But these renamings trigger other mutations and renamings, such that the sequence as a whole may be read as "*the creation of a multiple trace*" (136). Thus Jacob is renamed, the place is renamed, and a new taboo (against eating the sinew of the thigh) is established. These three renamings are "homological," having essentially the same structure (136). What we may note, then, is that the scene concludes with the "activity of language," and the "transgression of the rules of meaning" (136). This proliferation of names, traces, and meaning confirm the preceding reading of the story as one of the emergence of language. What Barthes has demonstrated, in each reading, is how the structure of the text is not neatly closed and confined. Not only is the text not orderly with some clear and definitive meaning, but the structure actually generates meaning in some ways. Thus the passage, which explicitly concerns the emergence of new names, enacts the generation of new meanings as a kind of allegory of its ostensible sequence.

Barthes concludes the essay by considering two basic approaches to structural analysis. The first is that associated with Algirdas Greimas, who argued that characters are actants around which action sequences are assembled—this was an argument Barthes discussed in the preceding essay. If we approach Jacob and God from this perspective, viewing the names of characters as a means of assembling action positions, we see that Jacob is the subject, the receiver, and the helper, while God is in the position of the sender and the opponent (137-38). This is significant because the combinations are not only dense (Jacob and God have multiple positions in the narrative), but because the actantial combinations are unexpected. As Barthes notes, "[t]he actantial form of the text" is "structurally,... extremely audacious—which squares well with the 'scandal' represented by God's defeat" (138). Here is a case, then, where structural analysis does not show how meaning is ordered, but can help us locate places where meaning diverges in some way.

The same is true with the "functional analysis" associated with the Russian formalist Vladimir Propp, who, in *Morphology of the Folktale*, had identified thirty-one "*functions* or narrative acts" (138). All Russian folktales, he argued, were comprised of different combinations of some of these thirty-one functions. One could productively map out the Genesis passage along the lines of Propp's folktale morphology, and Barthes notes several of the parallels that are possible (139-40). As with an exploration of Greimas's mode of structural analysis, what one would discover is that God, within these functions, is given "the role of the Villain" (140). It is not that God is here given the indicial attributes of a villain, but that God appears in the functions in "the *structural* role" of the villain (140). Once again, a structural analysis helps us locate what is most unusual— "audacious"—about the text in question, and why it provokes certain interpretive acts.

What Barthes has attempted to outline, throughout the essay, is a next step beyond the structural analysis outlined in the previous essay. This next step begins with "the structural exploitation of the episode" (140), to see how the structure is unusual, overladen, or compressed. In such cases, we find not a smoothly unfolding narrative of limited interpretive possibilities, but a series of "abrasive frictions," "breaks," and "discontinuities of readability" (140). These are moments where "the juxtaposition of narrative entities" breaks free from the rules of "an explicit logical articulation" (140), and it does this less by simple deviation but by a compression or combination of structural elements. This is what Barthes means when he speaks of the "*metonymic montage*" that is found in the Genesis passage: the different sequences are metonymic, since they signal other larger narrative conventions, but they operate formally as montage because they are overlapping and pressed together (140). In sum, he has moved his approach to the text much closer to his reading of the image in "The Third Meaning," and accordingly he ends the essay talking about reading practices that leave *"signifiance* fully open" (141). What we want to do, in reading, is explore not the stable meanings of a text reduced "to a signified," but to see the ways in which "the symbolic explosion of the text" occurs and can be explored (141). This "dissemination" of the text—the way it produces meanings from its active signifiers—may be at odds with "economico-historical" readings (141), but our task in *textual* reading is to move away from a reading of what the text means, and toward a reading of how the text generates meaning.

7. The Death of the Author

This short, experimental essay—comprised of six fragments of under 3,000 words—may be Barthes' best-known work. It first appeared in English in 1967, in the experimental, multimedia journal *Aspen*, published in the United States; the following year it appeared in the experimental French journal *Mantéia*. Three years later, in 1970, Barthes published a book titled *S/Z*, which is, among other things, a close reading of the novella "Sarrasine" by the nineteenth-century French realist writer Honoré de Balzac (1799-1850). There, Barthes attempts to lay out and demonstrate a new practice of reading competing tendencies in Balzac's story. "The Death of the Author," which begins and ends with references to the same story by Balzac, gives us some sense of how he was approaching this problem. Though the essay seems remote from "Introduction to the Structural Analysis of Narrative" in both style and substance, it is closer in interest than it may appear. For one thing, this manifesto-like piece accepts the complex view of the text developed in "Structural Analysis," and extends the critique of the author figure that appeared in the discussion of narration. This essay also extends the argument of "The Struggle with the Angel" toward what Barthes had called "textual criticism." It also finds a complement in another manifesto of a few years later, "From Work to Text."

Barthes begins with a sentence from Balzac's story, which it may help to consider in a slightly broader context. Here I have italicized the sentence singled out for analysis by Barthes:

> That morning fled too quickly for the enamored sculptor, but it was filled with a host of incidents which revealed to him the coquetry, the weakness, and the delicacy of this soft and enervated being. *This was woman herself, with her sudden fears, her irrational whims, her instinctive worries, her impetuous boldness, her fussings, and her delicious sensibility.* It happened that as they were wandering in the open countryside, the little group of merry singers saw in the distance some heavily armed men whose manner of dress was far from reassuring. Someone said, "They must be highwaymen," and everyone quickened his pace toward the refuge of the Cardinal's grounds. At this critical moment, Sarrasine saw from La Zambinella's pallor that she no longer had the strength to walk; he took her up in his arms and carried her for a while, running. When he came to a nearby arbor, he put her down.

In this scene, Sarrasine, the "enamored sculptor," is in the early days of wooing his new love interest, the singer La

Zambinella, who readers later discover is a castrated man dressed as a woman. We may immediately contextualize Barthes' choice of sentence in relation to his earlier essays on texts. We may note, for example, that Barthes has extracted one sentence surrounded by plot details—the fleeing morning, the countryside walk, the encounter with strange men, and Sarrasine's carrying of La Zambinella. The choice of sentence thus affirms Barthes' argument that narrative sequences provide the horizontal foundation for narrative, pushing it along. In this case, he selects a sentence more readily classified as narration—a higher level of integrational analysis—to explore how meaning works in the text.

Barthes asks who the speaker of this quotation is, and then proceeds to give five possible answers, which we must also consider. The first answer—"the hero of the story bent on remaining ignorant of the castrato hidden beneath the woman"—seems to follow from the narrative action, since the paragraph opens with Sarrasine's revelations. One might therefore say that this is Balzac manipulating his character, creating a misunderstanding in order to keep the plot moving. The second—"Balzac the individual, furnished by personal experience with a philosophy of Woman"—offers in shorthand the common view that either the narrator is the author, or, if we prefer, the central character voicing the sentiments of the author. The third answer—"Balzac the author professing 'literary' ideas on femininity"—again asserts the importance of the author, but with a refinement: here Balzac offers not his ideas, but adopts literary conventions or expectations about women. The fourth—"universal wisdom"—attributes these views to social context, understood as what everyone (in 1830

France) thinks. The fifth—"Romantic psychology"—*also* attributes these views to social context, but now understood in a narrower sense, that of one ideological current of early nineteenth-century France (Romanticism) as it intersects with one discipline (psychology) (142). In either case, Balzac is understood as a vehicle for the conveyance of historical context: he either presents a general or a specific ideology of his time, depending on how we locate him. In other words, we are given five types of analysis reliant on the author figure, whether based on (a) the author's structuring of the narrative text, (b) the author's biographical experience and opinions, (c) the author's literary environment and sense of him- or herself as a writer, or (d) social context, whether understood broadly (a universal belief) or (e) narrowly (one strand of belief among others).

Barthes' answer to his question—"Who is speaking thus?"—is then quickly given: "We shall never know" (142). Why? Because "writing is the destruction of every voice, of every point of origin" (142). And he continues: "Writing is that neutral, composite, oblique space where our subject slips away, the negative where all identity is lost, starting with the very identity of the body writing" (142). This is not an explanation as much as an assertion, although the next section of the essay provides some elaboration. "As soon as a fact is *narrated* no longer with a view to acting directly on reality but intransitively, that is to say, finally outside of any function other than that of the very practice of the symbol itself, this disconnection occurs, the voice loses its origin, the author enters into his own death, writing begins" (142). We saw an earlier version of this argument at the end of "Introduction to the Structural Analysis of Narrative," where Barthes argued for a reading of narrative as the creative expression of language in the intransitive—that is, not trying to communicate or achieve something, but demonstrating its nature as language. Here he takes this argument a step further, defining this kind of language "writing" in the proper sense. We might say that his argument here is that the removal of a clear destination for language (the transitive aim) therefore cuts off the origin point (the writer) and allows the language to have some kind of life of its own. But we will return to this answer after considering the rest of this essay.

The second section (142-43) focuses its attention on the historical cult of the author figure. If we consider narrative across history, we will not find the author significant in most historical moments. In more traditional societies (which Barthes calls "ethnographic"), authorship would have been an absurd concept; it was more common to think of the narrative as an expression of some narrative code outside of people, to be taken up "by a mediator, shaman or relator" (142). This last figure might be admired for his or her "performance," but would not be given credit for the creation of the narrative from some innate "genius" (142). In fact, authorship is a more recent phenomenon taking shape after the Middle Ages, and emerged from multiple influences. English empiricism, French rationalism, and Reformation theology all emphasized the isolated sensual body, consciousness, and soul, and thus all contributed to the idea of the human person as an individual, as opposed to a member of a collective (143). This notion of the author has thereafter been reaffirmed in countless ways—in literary histories, which focus on "great" individuals; in literary biographies and magazine profiles; in interviews with writers about their craft; and in the collections of letters, diaries, and memoirs assembled to provide background about the author at work (143). One might also think about the headnotes of anthologies, which always introduce a piece of writing with some information about the author figure's background. It is not surprising, then, notes Barthes, that we understand many artworks in terms of the artist's "person," "life," "tastes," or "passions" (143). The tendency to sum up and explain a work of art through some biographical detail (like Van Gogh's "madness" or Tchaikovsky's sexuality) is ubiquitous, Barthes claims (143). In this way, the work of art is always viewed somehow as an allegory about the author, as if the work is the author's way of "'confiding' in us" (143).

Barthes thus presents the focus on the author figure as both historical anomaly—the concept was not always important—and as a self-perpetuating belief—confirmed by the way we write and think about literature in scholarship or popular culture. But the next section of the manifesto talks about how the figure of the author has begun to break down in recent decades. Barthes first looks to several writers— Stéphane Mallarmé, Paul Valéry, Marcel Proust, and the surrealist movement—to find signs that even so-called "authors" understand the limitations of the author concept. Mallarmé, for instance, wrote poetry that foregrounded the dynamics of language itself—"it is language which speaks, not the author" (143). In fact, Mallarmé's "entire poetics consists in suppressing the author in the interests of writing" (143). Valéry, writing after Mallarmé, was less critical of the individual ego but nonetheless understood his writing through the lens of an older classical tradition in which a system of rhetoric took priority over the author (143-44). In his writings, he stressed "he essentially verbal condition of literature, in the face of which all recourse to the writer's interiority seemed to him pure superstition" (144). Marcel Proust, in his massive *In Search of Lost Time*, also blurred the author/narrator distinction by depicting an author figure only able to write once the epic text has ended (144). What's more, "instead of putting his life into his novel, as is so often maintained, he made of his very life a work for which his own book was the model" (144). Finally, the surrealist movement "contributed to the desacrilization" of the author figure by following strategies to disrupt "expectations of meaning" (144). For example, it refined a practice of "automatic writing" (writing so quickly with the hand as to move faster than consciousness) as well as routines for writing by multiple people (the "Exquisite Corpse" exercise) to undermine notions of authorial control.

Some have argued that this line of argument undermines Barthes' own claims about the death of author. After all, aren't these examples all examples that *reinforce* the idea of the author? Mallarmé, Valéry, Proust, the surrealists— weren't these all *authors* pushing their own versions of language? Didn't their suppression of authorship depend on an authorial decision? But Barthes' argument is not that the writer is irrelevant, but rather that the author figure as a critical fiction—whether for writers as they write, or for readers as they read—misleads and distorts, by shifting our focus from language to a person. These writers, then, do not disprove Barthes' argument, but are meant to illustrate how even writers increasingly understand, better than their predecessors, that the process of writing is not controlled by an author figure. What these more recent writers appreciate, in fact, is a point also increasingly made by linguists, who argue that "the whole of the enunciation is an empty process," not dependent on speakers (145). What this means is that the rules of language and the dynamics of syntax transcend individuals. If I articulate a sentence with the pronoun "I," that sentence will first of all follow the linguistic rules of a first-person sentence, will draw on signifiers with already established meaning, will follow rules of syntax, and so on. It is not a pure expression of my subjectivity, but rather a linguistic dynamic in which I am a participant through the "very enunciation," the act of speaking. Language "hold[s] together" the sentence, not I (145). It was this same linguistic insight that Mallarmé, Valéry, and the other mentioned writers understood and appreciated.

Accordingly, we might think about a different way of viewing writing with the "removal" or the "distancing" of the author figure (145). For one thing, our temporal sense of the modern text would change dramatically. With the author in mind, we will think of the book in terms of "a *before* and an *after*," with the author on the side of before (145). The author "*nourish[es]*" the book, "exists before it, thinks, suffers, lives for it," and is essentially the parent of the book (146). However, with the aforementioned linguistic understanding—that the text is the unfolding of language—we will approach the text differently. To imagine this alternative reading, Barthes introduces an alternative concept to describe the writer, the "scriptor," one who inscribes language on the page. This "gesture of inscription" should be contrasted with the sense that the author, as a full subject, *expresses* him- or herself; this belief in "expression" rather than "inscription" still adheres to the *before* of the author figure (146). The scriptor would not be the parental author-figure, but would instead emerge "simultaneously with the text" (145). We should appreciate that *scriptor* is not simply a different name for an author; what is involved in the concept of the scriptor is a different sense of the writing process in relation to the writer. The scriptor does not exist in any meaningful way before the writing, but comes into existence through the interplay with language. Writing in this respect is not "an operation of recording, notation, representation, [or] 'depiction'" (145), but is instead a "performative" act. Barthes offers a few examples of the performative mode of language—for example, the way ancient poets frequently began their works with "*I sing...*" or the way monarchs would make statements beginning "*I declare...*" (146). In these cases, the linguistic act declares what it is as it unfolds—the performance of a kind of language. The scriptor, says Barthes, operates in this performative mode, and the writing of the scriptor "has no other content...than the act by which it is uttered" (146).

The next section develops what might be considered broader philosophical implications of the author/scriptor opposition. What is at stake in the commitment to the author figure is an attitude toward language that is fundamentally "theological" (146). Barthes here develops an argument that was implicit in his reading of the Jacob story in Genesis: his analysis of the textual richness of biblical writing was opposed to the exegete's desire for a clear, decisive interpretation. In "The Death of the Author," such a religious attitude—an insistence on a single clear meaning—becomes a metonymy for a misguided approach to language more generally. By such a view, the writer is an "Author-God" (146), all texts are sacred and have a fixed meaning, and interpretation is an act of willful devotion opposed to textual analysis, which should be understood as "an anti-theological activity" (147). In fact, the text is not unified but is a "multi-dimensional space" of other writings "drawn from the innumerable centres of culture" (146). As a result, the scriptor is never a figure who creates something totally "original" (146). Rather, the scriptor "mix[es] writings" and "counter[s] the ones with the others" as a kind of mixer or sampler (146). The scriptor is thus more of a dee-jay than an oracle. As for what the "author" imagines to be "inside" him- or herself, it is "only a ready-formed dictionary" (146). The "passions, humours, feelings, [and] impressions" (147) we attribute to authors are actually textual elements from those different "centres of culture." The scriptor draws on them like a "copyist" (146), producing a "tissue" of "imitations" (147).

The penultimate section then addresses the implications of these claims about the author for criticism. Barthes notes that "the reign of the Author has also been that of the Critic" (147), as if the latter is the mirror image of the former. The traditional critic adheres to the author concept because it "impose[s] a limit," fixed parameters of interpretation (147). The critic, locating the Author in his or her time, will then have "*deciphered*" author and text with reference to personal experience, social context, or historical background, attaining the valuable underlying meaning. The goal in such an approach is like a "victory"—the definitive reading (147). To carry forth the theological allegory, this critic is like the priest claiming mastery of the "secret" of scripture (147). What we need, by contrast, is an alternative criticism that rejects the task of deciphering, understanding its proper activity to be "disentangl[ing]" (147). In other words, the critic should be looking at the different strands of writing woven through the text "like the thread of a stocking" (147). What the critic would then discover is not a catalogue of different elements, however. Remember the argument of "The Struggle with the Angel"—the textual critic seeks out dense spots in the text to see how they generate meaning. This is what Barthes intimates when he describes "writing" (now a better term than "literature") as something that "ceaselessly posits meaning ceaselessly to evaporate it" (147). This dual movement—positing *and* evaporating—is crucial. We are not simply seeking a more complex way of reading the text with more variables and sources. The problem of Balzac's sentence is not solved by combining all the possible answers, as if to say four or five interwoven answers were better than one. Barthes' point, instead, is that the intersections of strands both create and dissipate meaning, which comes and goes. Imagine the conjunction of two textual strands provoking a particular interpretation; then imagine a third strand undermining your fleeting sense of meaning; then imagine a fourth strand suggesting yet a different meaning, with a fifth strand disrupting that. And so on: it is this interplay, the flashing of meaning, that the new type of critic is trying to locate, however ephemerally it may occur. Only this way does the critic finally refuse "hypostases"—static meanings—modeled on God, reason, science, and law (147).

The final section of the manifesto takes the logical next step. If the author needs to be redefined (as a scriptor), so too does the critic. This new term? Simply enough, it is "the reader" (148). Barthes cites studies of the "constitutively ambiguous nature of Greek tragedy" (148), showing that much of the genre's language has multiple meanings; the experience of the tragedy comes from the combined effect of characters understanding only one meaning, while readers understand more than one. The tragedy readers encounter, then, is the false sense of a single meaning among characters in the text (148-49). Greek tragedy is thus a metonymy for writing in general, as it correctly locates the "multiple writings," the mutual relations of "dialogue, parody, [and] contestation" *in the reader* (148). The reader in this view is not an organizing, deciphering critic, but a "space" or a "destination" holding together "in a simple field all the traces by which the written text is constituted" (148). Those who attack difficult modern writing because it is too hard for readers are hypocritical, Barthes insists: the idea of accessibility and simplicity assumes a genius Author and a passive reader not worthy of respect. In fact, the active reader is where language can survive—the "death of the Author" implies "the birth of the reader" (148), which might be an alternative title to this piece. Where does this leave us with Balzac's sentence? "No one" says that sentence, if we are looking for outside sources and a clear meaning (147). But the ultimate answer is actually "the reader." For the sentence becomes significant—signifiant, to use the language of "The Third Meaning"—within the reader, who can see and enact the clashing of its different strands. Ultimately, then, reading is not about encountering a fixed thing and unlocking it once and for all, but about an approach to the text that keeps the dynamism of language open and apparent. For this to happen, we must assert "the death of the author," one of reading's biggest obstacles.

8. Musica Practica

This essay, the first of two treating music, appeared in 1970 in the French literary journal *L'Arc*. In this essay, we will find Barthes again challenging the conventions of interpretation associated with the nineteenth century and traditional approaches to art. In some respects, this is the argument of "Diderot, Brecht, Eisenstein" or "Death of the Author" applied to music, but there is an added dimension to the argument as well, one that turns our attention toward the bodily aspects of interpretation.

The essay begins with the opposition between "two musics"—"the music one listens to" and "the music one plays" (147). These two musics, Barthes says, are basically two "totally different arts," with different aesthetics, different social conditions, and different sensualities. What explains the difference between these two musics? The music of performance is essentially "manual" more than "auditory": if one plays piano, guitar, or any other instrument, one is focused on adjusting one's body to play the piece well, and one is more attuned to the demands of the performance than to the sound that results from this performance (149). Hence this is a "muscular music," by which Barthes means physically demanding, requiring the muscles to adjust and move. Thus it is "as though the body were hearing—and not 'the soul'" (149). "[S]eated at the keyboard or the music stand, the body controls, conducts, co-ordinates, having itself to transcribe what it reads, making sound and meaning, the body as inscriber and not just transmitter, simple receiver" (149). This last point is particularly important: the body making music is not a transmitter of the music; she does not passively translate the brilliance of the composer into sound, so others may hear that composer. Rather, the performer here is actually producing the music. This tradition of "musica practica"— the practice of making music—has "disappeared," says Barthes. It used to be the behavior of the aristocratic class, and later became a "social rite" among the bourgeoisie, who would gather for conventional performances in the drawing room (149). Since that time, the practice has almost died out, though Barthes acknowledges that a different strand of *musica practica* has emerged from "another public, another repertoire, another instrument"—namely, youth culture's practice of forming garage or basement rock bands.

Meanwhile, the other kind of music is "passive, receptive music" or "sound music" (149). Mass culture has made this kind of music overwhelmingly dominant. Performance has faded away, and music has accordingly changed in its nature, become "liquid" and "effusive"—the expression of some emotions or feelings (the composer's "heart" or "soul") that washes over us (150). This shift to passive music has entailed a change in performance as well. While the old manual music was performed by an amateur combining her own style with the occasional "technical imperfection," the new "sound music" is performed by "professionals, pure specialists" who execute the perfect performance. This will be a greater concern in Barthes' second music essay, "The Grain of the Voice," but here he notes that such virtuoso performances provide a sense of satisfaction, while the older performance style would trigger a "desire to *make* that music" (150). In sum, the modern music experience is "passive" in part because of the expertise of the "technician" (150), whose performance "relieves the listener of all activity" (150). Music thus increasingly becomes not a sphere of "*doing*," but of receiving (150).

Barthes will return to the ideal of *musica practica* at the end of the essay, but the bulk of it explores the significance of the German composer Ludwig van Beethoven (1770-1827). Barthes does not argue that Beethoven is somehow a "straightforward expression of a particular moment," but rather that the career of Beethoven expresses some of the divergent tendencies of music in the nineteenth and twentieth centuries (150). More precisely, Beethoven has "two historical roles," one "mythical," the other "modern" (150). Between these two roles, we can see some of the elements of the problem of musical experience, both as they find disruption and as they move toward a solution. Some sense of Beethoven's career, at least as it has been a subject of popular fascination, will be helpful here. Beethoven is best known for his large orchestral compositions, specifically the nine symphonies he composed between 1799 and 1824. His third symphony, the "Eroica" dedicated to Napoleon, has generally been considered his first original symphonic composition, meaning that he broke from the "classical" symphonic structure commonly associated with Haydn and Mozart. His later symphonies increasingly moved toward what has been called a Romantic style, with the four (sometimes five) movements "logically" presenting and resolving musical problems: one can hear this in the sequence through the four movements of his most famous symphony, the fifth. The later symphonies, while sharing a style commonly called "Romantic," are also quite distinct from one another, often experimenting with movement structure and length, or requiring larger groups of performers (like the ninth symphony, which required the largest assemblage of instruments as well as a chorus with four soloists). One could tell the story of Beethoven in any number of ways (discussing non-symphonic compositions, or different music-theoretical innovations, or his social position), but this synopsis is one of the narratives that has popularly defined Beethoven, and which Barthes takes up.

The first of Barthes' two Beethovens, then, is the mythical figure who "was the first man of music to be *free*" (150). He was the first major musician to move through "several successive *manners*"—the aggressively romantic manner of the fifth, the pastoral manner of the sixth, the playful manner of the eighth, and so on (150). The image thus emerged of the musician "in search of his 'truth'" (151), moving through styles not simply to experiment but in the search for more expressive music. As Barthes notes, Beethoven's "quest forms an order in itself, a message that can be read, in spite of the variations in its content, over all the work" (141). The result of this view of the musician as dynamic romantic is the emergence of a "bio-mythology" about Beethoven, complete with a "discourse" about Beethoven's style, a "legend" of Beethoven (anecdotes that recur in biographies and popular lore), an "iconography" (the famous glaring portraits of the composer), associations with other artists (like Michelangelo or Balzac), and even a "fatal malady" (Beethoven's gradual, ironic deafness) (151). There emerged then a view of Beethoven as "the symbol of restlessness and the seething agitation of creativeness" partly drawing on the dramatic shifts in his music (for example, the jump from loudness to softness, or the final use of choral music in the ninth) (151).

This "romantic image" of Beethoven poses a certain problem for a culture of performance, or *musica practica* (152). For one thing, since we are increasingly focused on complex symphonic works rather than songs or pieces written for the piano, the "amateur is unable to master Beethoven's music" (152). Indeed, so complex is the music that a new fantasy begins to emerge, that of the conductor or the *maestro* of the orchestra (152). Instead of imagining oneself playing individual instruments, one imagines oneself at the podium directing this section, then that section. In this way, the "body strives to be total," abandons the idea of the "amateur" performer, and shifts to a new sense of the listener as "the interpreter" (152). The problem with this view, of course, is that it kills the traditional *musica practica*. The performer is displaced by a combination of conductor and romantic empath, both outside the music in important ways. Paradoxically, this new model of the musician undermines our physical, practical participation in music.

Yet there is a concurrent counter-trend in the cult of Beethoven, grounded in the great irony of his deafness (152). This image of the deaf Beethoven composing symphonies invites still a different sense of music, one full of "signification" (152). We sense that music becomes a different substance for Beethoven, a "tangible intelligibility" (153). It is not sensual music, nor is it purely abstract, a matter of logic or rules. Rather, we imagine Beethoven combining the intelligible and the tangible in the written music, the score, where he becomes an "operator, who knows how to displace, assemble, combine, fit together," in short "who knows how to structure" music (153). With this second Beethoven, the deaf musician for whom ideas and sounds have converged, as a model, we too may develop the sense of a new engagement with music, "*operat[ing]*" it, "to draw it…into an unknown *praxis*" (153). Thus, while the mythological Beethoven signals the eclipse of the old *musica practica*, the "modern" Beethoven—the operator— shows how we might turn to a newer *musica practica*. This new engagement with music would render us composers in a revised sense—not "*giv[ing] to do*" or "to hear" in a passive way, "but to give to write" (153). What would this actually mean? For starters, imagine the stage on which musicians perform, and passing "from one source of sound to another" (153). Then imagine an extension of this concert as a kind of "workshop, from which nothing spills over"—that is, where the full range of musical production is experienced and not edited or censored (154). This would be something like Barthes' "utopia" of the "future" (154).

We will have to admit that this utopia is certainly hard to grasp, but we may at least see parallels here with the kind of free play of reading described in "The Death of the Author" or of viewing treated in "Diderot, Brecht, Eisenstein." What is envisioned here is an active listening that at least makes sense as an ideal, if still unclear as a practice. In fact, this might be the most useful reading of "Musica Practica": music is taken up as a different medium through which to test Barthes' changing, increasingly prescriptive approach to language. We will see one additional engagement with music in "The Grain of the Voice," and an analogue to the workshop utopia in "Writers, Intellectuals, Teachers," but here we may note one important addition to Barthes' program—the bodily side of interpretation. Barthes began his essay describing an idea of the old *musica practica*— feeling music physically by performing. As we have seen, Barthes is skeptical about reviving this "naive" sensuality, which will not be "authentic" but culturally determined. People who try to "get into" music (for example, by closing their eyes, by moving their bodies in certain ways, etc.) are not communing with music, but rather are imitating the conventions of music listening. What we must attempt, rather, is an engagement with music at once attuned to the dynamics of performance *and* listening *and* instrument.

Remember Barthes' claim, in "The Death of the Author," that "there is one place where this multiplicity" of writings "is focused and that place is the reader" (148). The same argument holds here for music, and given the obvious sensual dimensions of music, we may say that there is one place where this multiplicity of musical elements is focused, and that place is the listener's body. In other words, we are called on to understand the encounter with music as intellectual, yes, but physical as well—in other words, the sensual and the conceptual encounters with music will coincide. We will see this insistence on the physical side of interpretation become more and more important in Barthes' writing.

9. From Work to Text

From the late 1960s into the early 70s, Barthes wrote a series of manifesto pieces announcing the shift in his criticism from structuralist analysis of the working of signs to what has come to be called "poststructuralism." Poststructuralism exists in many different forms, and Barthes' writings constitute only one variant, if an influential one. But as it emerged as a movement—and we see, in this piece, the attempt to define a broader philosophical movement—a number of theorists, Barthes included, published programmatic statements describing the new approach. "The Third Meaning," "Diderot, Brecht, Eisenstein," "The Death of the Author," and "Musica Practica" are all pieces in this vein, as is "From Work to Text," which appeared in 1971 in the journal *Révue d'esthétique*. The experimental nature of these manifestos is apparent: unlike the more structuralist essays ("The Photographic Message," "Rhetoric of the

Image," and "Introduction to the Structural Analysis of Narrative"), these essays are more tentative in their claims, with long meandering sentences full of parenthetical asides, colons and semi-colons, lists, and neologisms. These are all deliberate innovations intended to illustrate the very arguments Barthes is making: the challenges of following Barthes' sentences demonstrate the new kind of reading he promotes. We have seen the emergence of this new reading most explicitly in "The Struggle with the Angel," "The Third Meaning," and "The Death of the Author," which focused on textuality, significance, and the reader respectively. "From Work to Text" attempts to be more programmatic in announcing a fundamental conceptual shift from the old-fashioned concept of the literary "work" to the newer dynamic experience of the "text." As a call to a new way of thinking, this piece moves away from an analysis based on an example, which makes it more challenging to read. As Barthes says, what he offers here is a series of propositions not so much "in a logical sense" but as "enunciations": in other words, these are not so much traditional "argumentations" as they are "touches," reflections on a new style of thought (156).

But it should be added that Barthes does not believe he is simply an avant-garde theorist announcing a new agenda for the sake of its newness. As he admits at the outset, what he describes here is not a sharp epistemological break, a dramatic rupture announcing a new paradigm. Rather the propositions he offers are part of a long-term "epistemological slide" influenced by changes in a number of disciplines, including "linguistics, anthropology, Marxism and psychoanalysis" (155). These disciplines, it is important to add, are not moving in synch, not doing the same thing with the same insights and the same results. For that reason, when Barthes talks about "interdisciplinarity," the relationship between different disciplines of study, he is not assuming agreement and coordination, but rather "encounter[s]" around a common object—the text— that is not the proper subject matter of any of them (155). What he assumes, then, is less shared insights among these disciplines than some common themes that emerge from their "confrontation[s]," as traditional disciplines break down. This breakdown has been happening for at least a century—remember the references to older writers in "The Death of the Author," or the discussion of Beethoven in "Musica Practica"—such that the last hundred years has produced a series of "repetition[s]" all striving toward similar conclusions. At the heart of this "repetition" (155) is a rethinking of the relationship between "writer, reader and observer (critic)," all positions defined by their further relationship to a common object, the text (156). The realignment of these three terms around a fourth demands a redefinition of the object of study, now called "the *Text*" (156). The Text will accordingly be examined through seven different lenses, as if to offer a series of theses on our current historical situation.

Method. The section on method appears at first to be more concerned with a definitional problem—what are "works" and what are "texts"? Barthes wants to challenge the avant-gardist view that the stodgy old literature of the past—what we often call "classic" writing—are works, while modern writing, of a different sort, now consists of texts. In fact, the two are not distinct, and it "would be futile to try to separate out materially works from texts," based on their historical moment (156). One can find the text "in a very ancient work," while much contemporary writing may be read as works (156). What we must understand is that "text" and "work" are two different *perspectives*. The text is a "methodological field," a "process of demonstration" that we perceive in "the movement of discourse" (157). As Barthes summarizes it, *"the Text is experience only in an activity of production"* (157). A work, by contrast, is not a different thing but a different attitude, one that views the writing as settled and determined, fixed on the page and mounted on a shelf in the library. As the old witticism goes, a classic is a book everyone respects and no one reads. But a text may be the same book actively read. We have seen this argument before, in the discussion of the passive film viewing vs. the actively read still ("The Third Meaning"), the passive drama vs. the active staging ("Diderot, Brecht, Eisenstein"), passive listening vs. active, sensual composing ("Musica Practica"), or exegetical interpretation vs. the search for signifiance ("The Struggle with the Angel"). So what appears initially as a definitional problem is actually one of attitude, perspective, and method. The *Text* implies a specific approach and agenda.

Genre. Could we therefore locate the text in certain complex genres (the novel, the poem) and the work in other, stiffer literary modes (the didactic essay, or genre fiction like the detective story or romance)? In other words, does text correspond in some way with standard literary classifications of genre? The answer is no. Barthes gives a few examples here. One is *La Vie de Rancé* (*The Life of Rancé*) by François-René de Chateaubriand (1768-1848), which at first glance would be classified as a religious biography, certainly not a dynamic text. In fact, this old work is a text because it "goes to the limit of the rules of enunciation," and thus draws our attention to the "activity of production" (157). This makes it what the French critic Albert Thibaudet (1875-1936) called a "limit-work," a work that pushes the recognized boundaries of genre. Barthes' other example is the writing of George Bataille (1897-1962), an experimental theorist who wrote in a wide range of genres. To classify Bataille according to the generic conventions he sometimes seemed to adopt would be misleading: it would make more sense to see Bataille's writings as "continuously one single text" (157), as the crux of his writing extends across the limits of genres. What we are seeking, in the text, is something that is literally "*paradoxical*" (158)—that is, contrary (*para-*) to fixed opinion (*-doxa*). And because generical classifications are a way of focusing on and emphasizing set norms or opinions of works, textual analysis must leave the old problem of genre behind. Again, we may recall here Barthes' reading of the Jacob story—what made it interesting was how it "paradoxically" defied the conventions of certain narrative sequences—or "Diderot, Brecht, Eisenstein," which seemed to begin as a reading of theatrical tableaus but then extended that argument to analogous moments in a wide range of artistic media, as if the medium itself was not important.

Signs. As we've seen, Barthes' work in the early 1960s was heavily influenced by the structuralist model of the sign as the relationship between signifier and signified. His earliest studies of the photograph had stressed the troubling ways in which the connotative signifieds dominated and mastered the denotative signifiers, as if in an unequal relationship. But "The Third Meaning" had shifted its attention to an interpretive strategy to arrest the power of the signified and to allow the signifier the freedom of signifiance. "The

Struggle with the Angel" had begun to extend this argument to texts as well, a project more clearly formulated here. The *work* characteristically "closes on a signified" (158), and in one of two ways—the signified is either deemed obvious and self-evident, or it is treated as a secret truth to be uncovered by the critic. Either way, the signified is something static. Returning to the point about "method," this means that any perspective on writing as text is committed to the stable signified, the stable sign, and thus the stable work itself (158). By contrast, the text focuses on the signifier and the "infinite deferment of the signified" (158). Barthes refines his argument a bit here: the point is not to focus on the signifier to the exclusion of the signified, but to recognize that the connection between the two is always delayed, plural, overlapping, uneven, variable. The complexity of the text, as hinted in "Introduction to the Structural Analysis of Narrative," is such that the signifier-signified relationship could and will take multiple paths. So while the signifier is not "infinite," it *plays* through a number of different relationships with the signified. If the work is "symbolic," then, it is only "*moderately*" so; the text, by contrast, is "*radically* symbolic" (158), because the signifier-signified relationship is so much more active and multi-dimensional. The text is thus like language in this respect—"structured but off-centred, without closure" (159). There is a humanist argument running in the background here as well. For the symbolic energy of the text is essential to human thriving— "lacking it, man would die," writes Barthes (158). And if theorists akin to Barthes have insisted that language is the foundation of epistemology, the science of knowledge, this is why: for knowledge to change and develop, it must be a "system with neither close nor centre" (159).

Plurality. This view of the open play between signifier and signified means that the text is therefore plural. And Barthes stresses that this does not mean that texts have multiple, coexisting meanings, nor that the meaning of the text is sometimes ambiguous and unclear. Rather, this plurality is "irreducible," like "an explosion" or "a dissemination" (159). Barthes likens the encounter with the text to a walk through a strange landscape, and that sense of the "unfamiliarity" from "a disconnected heterogeneous variety of substances and perspectives" (159). Here we may encounter "lights, colours, vegetation, heat, air, slender explosions of noises, scant cries of birds, children's voices from over on the other side, passages, gestures, clothes of inhabitants near or far away" (159). We may half-recognize these different stimuli on their own, we may recognize their codes, but we have never encountered this combination before, and have never tried to register this particular interplay of codes (159). Thus the plurality of the text will seem "*stereographic*," written from multiple directions (159). And he takes this image further in thinking about the endless relationships between texts, what we call *inter-textuality*. We must resist the view, common in literary histories, that texts are bound together by "filiation"— that is, one text influences another, which then informs another, and so on in a line of familial descent (160). This filiation is a "myth," for the real "sources" and "influences" of a work messily come from multiple directions, not in orderly pedigrees (160). The text is full of quotations without quotation marks—they are "anonymous, untraceable, and yet *already read*" (160). In a final metaphorical shift that harkens back to "The Death of the Author," Barthes suggests that the work, with its focus on a single meaning, is like an orthodox religion that can only view plurality as "Evil" (160). But the text is, in this view, "demoniacal," and one could quote the gospel of Mark as a motto for the text: "My name is Legion: for we are many" (160). To emphasize plurality then involves challenging any institution or school or movement (he includes a certain kind of marxism here) that is focused on "monism"—unified meaning (160).

Network. This next section takes up some of the arguments in "The Death of the Author," with some interesting twists and extensions. At first, it seems a reiteration of that essay. The falsely-conceived *work*, Barthes says, belongs to a "process of filiation," and seems clearly determined by world and history, conforming to a clear sense of the parental author (160). It is imagined to be like an "organism," closed and with a clear developmental history (161). What then is the text? The better metaphor would be one taken from information or transportation systems—"the *network*" (161). This means the text can be broken, interrupted, or stalled, read without any clear central point, or explored in terms of different combinations (161). But here we see Barthes modify the argument of his earlier manifesto. For if we connect the author figure with the text at all, it must not be as the creator or origin of the text but as a "guest" in the text's networks (161). One might say that the author is a "paper-author," his or her biography becoming another network strand contributing to the text. And in fact, we may go still one step further, reversing the terms. If the *author* was a way of thinking (wrongly) about the *work*, we may now say that the *text* offers a way of thinking (more productively) about the author concept. We need not abandon the author idea altogether, as was suggested in "The Death of the Author," but can now think about the author's life as a networked text itself: "bio-graphy" can be understood as the writing of life in the textual sense (161).

Reading. "The Death of the Author" had also stressed the shift from author to reader, and this piece now revises and extends that position as well, drawing on the argument of "Musica Practica." Barthes must first make clear what he does *not* mean by reading, and his attack is two-fold. Historically, he notes that in the past, elites were taught how to write—that is, they were encouraged to pursue an active mode of culture (162). With the democratic revolutions and the rise of mass education, however, students were taught to *"read"*—the passive acceptance of culture (162). As an aside, Barthes adds that the trend in writing classes to encourage students to "express themselves" is misguided: the imposed passivity or "repression" has been replaced by the "misconception" that students have a clear and personal something to express, when they should rather be taught active participation in culture (162). In another aside, Barthes notes that this passivity also explains the "boredom" many feel when faced with a difficult text; this boredom actually registers the passive reader's inability to figure out how to make the text signify (163). What has emerged, then—and this is Barthes' second critique—is a "consumer culture" of reading works as one would consume any other commodity (161). Some may delude themselves into thinking that they are discerning the "quality" of great literature, unlike the ignorant proles reading on the train (161-62). But the two modes, both passive consumption, are structurally identical (162).

What would active reading look like? Here Barthes rehearses the argument of "Musica Practica." Once "practising amateurs" combined "'playing' and 'listening,'" then this role diverged into professional, interpreting performers and passive listeners of recordings (162-63). But a new form of musical experience is emerging now, in which the "interpreter" is "called on to be in some sort the co-author of the score, completing it rather than giving it 'expression'" (163). This model is a good one for reading, and the text may be compared to a musical score of different parts and notations (163). The reader of the *text*, then, is a collaborator, engaged in "play, activity, production, practice" (162). We can think of the multiple meanings of "play" in this respect. The text *plays* like a machine or a door with some give; the reader *plays* as one might play a game, "looking for a practice which re-produces it" (162); but the reader also *plays* the text in a "musical sense," executing the text, or "*set[ting] it going*" (163). If we seek a model, we may look no further than this essay itself. As Barthes notes in the final paragraph, what he is attempting here is a playing of different strands "developed round about him" (164).

Pleasure. The musical analogue of reading-as-playing brings us finally to the experience of pleasure, which here takes a very specific form. There may be a certain kind of pleasure in "reading and re-reading" older works—he mentions Balzac, Dumas, Flaubert, and Proust (163). But here he comes close to contradicting his earlier claim that works are not old, texts not necessarily new. For whatever the pleasures this older literature might provide, there is no active pleasure. One cannot "*re-write*" those works, and must instead passively consume them (163). Why? Because they are pre-modern, and "clearly…cannot be started over again" (163-64). What, then, is the pleasure of the modern text? Barthes gives two answers, one negative, one positive. The new pleasure *cannot* be that of a "metalinguistic exposition," meaning we cannot develop theories (like that of "Introduction to the Structural Analysis of Narratives") that will explain the workings of the text. This is not active participation in the composition of the text. Rather, the new pleasure "should be nothing other than text, research, textual activity"—in short, participation *within* (not above or "outside") the text (164). Inside the text, our active reading will "coincide...with a practice of writing" (164). And there we will experience the special pleasure of "*jouissance*," which Barthes defines as "a pleasure without separation" (164). We will then be participating in a space of transparent "language relations," where no single "language has a hold over any other, where languages circulate" (164). This space of pleasure, *in language*, is our alternative, our parallel social space. We cannot experience this transparency or freedom in the social sphere—but we can in language, which becomes our new "utopia" (164). We might finally, then, add an eighth rubric—*politics*—noting that linguistic or textual analysis has largely abandoned the sphere of political struggle to the monists with clear answers. The textualists will find their freedom elsewhere, in an engagement with the text. We will explore this political shift in more detail with the next essay.

10. Change the Object Itself

Roland Barthes' career can usefully be read as an influential and illustrative case of French theory's transition from structuralism to poststructuralism, and the changing concerns we have seen emerge are very representative of broader shifts. The clear interpretive agenda of structuralism—the delineation of language's components, the systematic mapping of its dynamics, and the location of language's role in society—increasingly mutated into something very different—a fuzzier and more complicated sense of language, a prescriptive insistence on possible engagements with language, and a denial of the distinction between language and society. This last point was grounded in the increasing awareness that language was not one dimension of society but the omnipresent medium of society itself. The consideration of any social phenomenon was always undertaken within and through language. When Barthes, in "From Work to Text," argued against meta-analysis and in favor of working *in* and *through* the text, this was less a preference than an acknowledgment that meta-analysis was also an activity in language not legitimately treated as distinct. As we have seen, this shift also entailed a redefinition of the politics of criticism, and that is arguably the central topic of "Change the Object Itself," a 1971 essay in which Barthes returned to his 1957 *Mythologies* to offer a self-critique.

As discussed in the introduction, *Mythologies* had taken up semiotic analysis as a tool to debunk the ideological illusions of a class-biased bourgeois society—in sum, its political agenda was clearly on the left, and understood cultural analysis as an important moment in the critique of society and the effort to change it. Looking back on *Mythologies* "[s]ome fifteen years" later, however, how did Barthes summarize his earlier work? He outlines here four major points, before offering corrections or clarifications of these earlier positions.

The first of these was a belief in the "reflection" theory of culture. The mythologies Barthes described and debunked "reflected" beliefs held by society, but which found "anonymous" expression in the press, in advertising, and in a host of elements of popular culture (165). No individual or group created these myths—they were not the diabolical creations of bourgeois propagandists—but they somehow still expressed the state of society in an unattributable fashion (165). Second, the myth had an "inverted" structure, turning the social, historical, and cultural situations into something "natural" (165). Phenomena specific to a historical moment were perceived, "under the effect of mythical inversion," as timeless expressions of "Common Sense, Right Reason, the Norm, General Opinion"—all manifestations of a dominant cultural orthodoxy (165). The solution to this inversion was obviously to re-invert, to reestablish the priority of the historical and cultural against this false, universal naturalism. Third, "[c]ontemporary myth" was "discontinuous" and scattered, expressed not in long expository narratives but in scattered examples, "phrases," and objects. What this meant was that there was no single "myth" to attack, no master-narrative that required debunking, but a pervasive *"mythical"* quality to things that was much more "insidious" (165). Finally, the theoretical agenda of myth analysis, grounded in "semiology," understood signification in terms of "two semantic systems"—a "denoted system" of the "apparent literalness" of the thing in question, registered by the signifier, and the distorted "connoted system" of the signified (166). The task of semiology was to distinguish these two systems and reestablish the proper hierarchy of signifier over signified, reality over myth (166).

Such was the program in 1957. So where did things stand in 1971, after the proliferation of progressive left movements? "French society" had not really changed, nor had the myths Barthes had analyzed, which remained "just as anonymous and slippery, fragmented and garrulous" as before (166). But the "*science of reading*" had in the interim changed, Barthes insists, such that the myth has become essentially "*a different object*" (166). Here Barthes focuses on two major changes in the formulation of the problem. The first concerns the changing status of the signifier. We have seen this argument play out across Barthes' writing, in which the signifier goes from being the denotative marker of reality to a source of significance, intrinsically capable of generating different meanings. As a result, Barthes' older claims about the domination of the signifier by the signified have changed as well. Indeed, he argues that his earlier view of the dominant signifier and the denotative signified was itself "in some sort mythical" (166). The debunking of myths had become itself a "mythological doxa," a classroom activity carried out by any number of students as a kind of rote exercise complete with its own "stock of phrases" and "catechistic declaration" (166). But this exercise gets it wrong, for "the problem is not to reveal the (latent) meaning of an utterance, of a trait, of a narrative, but to fissure the very representation of meaning" (167). In other words, our goal should not be to brush aside the signified to get at the pure, solid signifier and its link to reality, but rather to rethink and disrupt the signifier-signified connection.

If the older critical mode was that of "mythoclasm," the shattering of myths, the new mode should instead be that of "semioclasm," the shattering of signs themselves (167). Such a program will be "much more far-reaching and pitched at a different level" (167). What we should be challenging, instead of specific myths about French culture or politics, is a general commitment to fixed meaning. If Barthes had hinted this belief in his theological metaphors, he is now explicit. The problem of the stable sign is endemic to "the whole of Western civilization," meaning the full "Graeco-Judaeo-Islamo-Christian" heritage. Classical and monotheistic cultures, Plato and the French newspaper, law and religion, the old views of art—all participate in the myth of the stable sign. Semioclasm therefore needs to be nothing less than a critique of western civilization. It will be obvious that Barthes' sense of politics has changed here. If he had once defined bourgeois domination within capitalism as the major political problem, it is now the western regime of the sign, which encompasses but also dwarfs class politics. Less evident may be Barthes' critique of the left itself. If the terminology of *Mythologies* was implicitly marxist, the marxist (and socialist, and communist) program is now a target, due to its naive desire to attack bourgeois ideology. In fact, the closing sentences' reference to Marx is less a renewed commitment to marxism than a warning: marxism had better develop itself around the new object, as a "new science" (169).

Hand in hand with the new semioclasm should be a new focus on "sociolects" (168). Once we complicate the signifier-signified relationship, we can ask "more syntactical" questions like "what are the articulations, the displacement, which make up the mythological tissue of a mass consumer society?" (167). In other words, we should explore the set modes and forms with which mass society again and again connects signifier and signified. The problem with the *Paris-Match* cover was not its specific endorsement of

French imperialism as much as it was the mass impulse to read the cover as an endorsement of imperialism. Barthes had introduced the concept of the "sociolect" in "The Photographic Message," where it referred to clusters of connotative associations (like the aesthete's familiarity with European artistic conventions). But here sociolect is a more abstract entity. Sociolects are "habits and repetitions,... stereotypes, obligatory final clauses and key-words" (168). In short, they are forms, patterns, of interpretation—and consequently deluded and harmful. The project of analyzing "sociolects" would be in part to identify *forms* of ideology, in part to counter actively common sociolexic tendencies. Because the "world is written through and through" by "signs, endlessly deferring their foundations," our critique should try to approximate this real state of language (167). Instead of myth-debunking, we should craft a new practice that is "airy, light, spaced, open, uncentred, noble and free" (168). So mutative and unstable would this practice be that we could not even really call it a sociolect, for it would never take a set form.

Thus Barthes' new agenda, so politically vague that he himself calls it an "inclination" rather than a "program" (169). We have to accept that the western world is shot through with "mythical speech"—it is in popular culture, literature, political life, even our thoughts—and we must be engaged in the critique of all aspects of the west. But we can no longer critique myth by *"upend[ing]"* it; rather we must develop new habits of language, behavior, and thought (169). We will see, in the final segments of *Image-Music-Text*, the extension of this argument. The next essay, "Lesson in Writing," tries to imagine a non-western form of interpretation, and "The Grain of the Voice" turns toward the bodily, sensual extension of this new "inclination" in one more discussion of music. But it is the last essay, "Writers, Intellectuals, Teachers," that most actively tries to imagine new forms of behavior, if only within the university system.

11. Lesson in Writing

We have seen, in Barthes' works, a number of attempts to explain and illustrate the new approach to language he advocates by the late 1960s and early 1970s. His account of music listening in "Musica Practica," of textual interpretation in "The Struggle with the Angel," of reading as being something like a walk in the countryside in "From Work to Text"—all struggled to clarify what a new interpretive approach might look like. Among the clearest of these examples was perhaps his account of theater in "Diderot, Brecht, Eisenstein," as he envisioned the reader/viewer focusing on specific elements of the play (the gest, the pregnant moment, the tableau, and so on). "Lesson in Writing" takes up a theatrical example once more, again as a kind of allegory of interpretation. Its specific subject is the *bunraku* theater of Japan, a dramatic form that thrived during the Tokugawa shogunate, and has persisted in recent centuries as a traditional form of theater. Japanese culture— mostly certain stylized elements of traditional Japanese culture—was the subject of Barthes' 1970 book *Empire of Signs*, which actually included several passages on *bunraku*; this essay, published in 1968, is an early draft version of arguments later presented in book form. Barthes' interest in Japanese culture resulted in part from several long visits in 1966-67, though he had also encountered theoretical engagements with Japanese theater in the work of Bertolt Brecht, whose work is mentioned several times in this essay. While Barthes disclaimed any expertise in speaking of Japan, and even eventually denied that he was writing about Japan—he was, he said, writing about his fantasy of Japan—it is clear that his interest stemmed in part from his curiosity about systems and rules of language outside of the West. So while this short piece explores an example of Japanese theater to present an alternative model of reading, it makes larger claims about "the West" and its persistent theoretical mistakes.

What, first of all, is *bunraku* theater? Barthes gives a nice clear description. Puppets, smaller than humans and with "moveable limbs, hands, and mouth," are manipulated by groups of three men visible to the spectators. While the three manipulators work different parts of the puppet, two other groups—musicians and narrators—stand apart to "*express*" the text, which is "half-spoken, half-sung" with "violence and artifice" (170). The speakers are visible behind daises, turning the pages of their script, as their faces are framed behind triangles of canvas (170). Barthes likes *bunraku* for the ways in which it challenges certain important western binaries or antitheses. "The West," he argues, is collectively a "culture" that fixates on such binaries, above all the opposition between "good and evil" (171). But there are two other binaries that comprise the target of this essay, before its final celebration of fragmentation.

The first of these is the distinction between the animate and the inanimate (171). At stake in this opposition is the clear definition of the human, understood as the unified body of the person, motivated by a central impulse (perhaps called the heart, the soul, the mind, the spirit, or whatever).

The clearest example of this appears with the method actor, who tries to take on the full complexity of his or her character from head to toe, with facial expressions, body language, gait, habits, and so on. Even the practice of ad-libbing, departing from the script, reinforces this idea, as such departures are presumed possible because the actor has fully embodied the character (177). Thus this acting style "borrows from physiology the alibi of an organic unity, the unity of 'life'" (171). In a similar way, the inanimate is confirmed by the western-style puppet. A stiff little caricature puppet like a Punch or a Judy is a degraded, mechanical version of a human, moving jerkily, erratically, like a thing or an "automaton" (172). Our perception of the puppet as a non-human depiction of human behavior, typically calling attention to human shortcomings, thus reinforces the idea of the animate. In the end, we are either fully animate (the actor figure) or we use clearly inanimate puppets. *Bunraku* disrupts this opposition by ridding us of the actor. It amounts to a "reflection on the human body...conducted by inanimate matter with infinitely more rigour and excitement than by the animate body" (171). The goal is not to animate the puppet, not to make it "the simulation of the body," but rather to turn the puppet into a kind of "concrete abstraction" (172). By foregrounding the human-puppet relationship, we focus on a composite attempt to capture elements of expressiveness, seeing, instead of persons or things, "fragility, discretion, sumptuousness, extraordinary nuance, abandonment of all triviality, melodic phrasing of gestures," all *qualities* of the body without the full body. By transferring these elements of "impassiveness, clarity, agility, [and] subtlety" to the puppet, the animate/inanimate distinction is overturned and refused. No one can maintain, in this theater, that "animation" results from the interior soul inside the body (172). In fact, this graceful animation of the inanimate calls attention to the awkward parts and pieces of the western actor's body (171).

The second and related opposition challenged by *bunraku* is that of inner vs. outer. In the case of persons, westerners imagine each individual has a rich "inner" life that takes place in consciousness, conscience, heart, soul, or so on. This interiority then finds expression in outward behaviors, or exteriority. Happiness becomes a smile, anger a scowl, anxiety certain bodily movements, and so on—"inner" life always finds an "outer" expression. Western norms of acting obviously reinforce this split—behaviors are read as outer signs of the character's inner state. In fact, the very structure of western theater reinforces this idea as well, as the stage often seems an inner or private space of the characters that we are secretly viewing (173). Meanwhile, all that points to the artifice of theater (make-up, lighting, special effects, painted backdrop, stage machinery) are typically hidden or veiled (173). *Bunraku* obviously disrupts this type of theatrical presentation—we see the manipulators doing their tasks, we witness the full apparatus of puppets and stage. Where we see the face of the primary puppet master, it is expressionless. Nor is the puppet the external manifestation of the main puppeteer, for there are others contributing to the performance. What we focus on then is "work" instead of interiority (173-74).

If we overlay these two binaries—animate/inanimate, and inner/outer—we see some correspondences (the inanimate is sometimes associated with the physical exterior, while animation is linked with one's inner being), and we find that they add up to a focus on the whole, the "illusion of totality" (174). Westerners need the binaries, in fact, to confirm their sense of how the whole works, and this sense of wholeness, grounded in the belief in the unified self, is projected onto the exterior world in the form of the "spectacle," the perception of the total drama. As Barthes notes, "Western spectacle is anthropomorphous"—its holistic quality comes from the western sense of the human (175). Much as westerners imagine the totality of their behavior and body, and the orderly connection between their interior and exterior lives, so too they see that unity on the western artistic production. We might take, as another example, the norms of western cinema—the giant screen, "surround-sound" overwhelming the audience, and, more recently, 3D—as signs of this love of and belief in the spectacle.

Again, *bunraku* disrupts this western norm, primarily by staging "three separate writings which are given for reading simultaneously in three areas" (175). There is the marionette, the embodied gesture; the manipulators, or the gestures that make the marionette move; and finally the "vociferator," who reads the script (175). The meaning thus comes from three different places. One might say, in fact, that while the western spectacle coordinates image, music, and text (staging, sound, and script), *bunraku* separates them, forcing the viewer to coordinate her reading of the performance, composing it herself. Furthermore, these isolated elements disallow complicity in the spectacle. Barthes' primary example here is the stylized voice of the speakers in the *bunraku* performance. Its display of "extravagant declamation, tremulous quiver, shrill feminine tones, broken intonations, tears, paroxysms of anger and lamentation, supplication and astonishment, [and] indecent pathos" is executed according to set norms, not some fantasy of the actor channeling the character (175). In addition, the verbal portion of the performance calls attention to the voice emerging from the "mediating muscle" of the vociferator's body (176). Expressions of emotion are not linked with contortions of face or body to simulate a person: "expelled from a body that remains motionless, mounted in the triangle of the costume, linked to the book which guides it from the lectern, studded sharply by the slightly off-phased…strokes of the [instrument] player, the vocal substance stays written, discontinued" (176). In this way, the voice is "set aside," as is the "gesture" of the puppet: the manipulations of the marionette are there for everyone to see (176).

Bunraku is thus unashamed theater, revealing without embarrassment how it comes about, unlike the "ashamed" theater of the west, hiding its mechanisms like dirty secrets (176). This openness, this revelation, can produce in viewers an "exaltation as special…as the intellectual hyperaesthesia attributed to certain drugs" (176-77). Such an art form is truly "revolutionary," says Barthes, because it "shows how it can function: by the discontinuity of codes" (177). More specifically, what emerges here is "the reign of the *quotation*" long ago sought by Bertolt Brecht—an experience of theater attentive to what it does, how it works, and where its elements come from linguistically (177). With such an approach, the richness of the text, with its "codes, references, discontinuous observations, anthological gestures," opens up, now on the stage (178). As we noted in our earlier treatment of "Change the Object Itself," Barthes moves toward a new politics that may be called experiential, one of a changed consciousness of the workings of language.

Bunraku here offers a metaphor of what that experience might look—or, better, feel—like. Whether or not it seems adequate can perhaps be tested by a thought experiment: imagine you are watching the "theater" of contemporary politics, and imagine that, instead of falling for it, taking it seriously, you recognize its mechanisms, its production of meaning, its various components interweaving different sociolects. If you cannot imagine yourself enjoying such an experience, it may be because this example is still one of aesthetic appreciation rather than engagement with the world to change it.

12. The Grain of the Voice

In his later writings, re-envisioning the criticism of any cultural medium, Barthes typically adopts two complementary strategies. One is a reformulation of the field of art, such that one's perceptions and understanding are transformed by its complexity, multiplicity, and diversity. We may think of the complex view of the stage in "Diderot, Brecht, Eisenstein," or "Lesson in Writing," or of the networked texts described in "The Death of the Author" and "From Work to Text." Alongside this strategy, Barthes often invites us to pinpoint particular elements and "change the object" of study itself, as in the essay of that name. Of the two music essays, "Musica Practica" emphasizes the former strategy, "The Grain of the Voice" the latter. For the project in this 1972 piece is to "change the musical object itself" (180). As we have seen, "Lesson in Writing" celebrated the Japanese "vociferator," the speaker who, in stylized, emotional performances, called attention to the voice as the site of cultural production. This essay extends that argument along the lines of "Change the Object Itself"—that is, by turning our attention from the composite thing (the myth in the former essay, "music" in general in this one) to the more precise location of signifiance. In "Change the Object Itself," that had been the dialectic between signifier and signified; here it is the *"encounter between a language and a voice,"* what Barthes calls the "grain" (181). This musical shift is particularly crucial because language's attempts to discuss music so consistently fall short, resorting to the "adjective" (179). Not knowing how to grasp the signification taking place within and through music, we give it a label ("moving," "upbeat," "punk," "heavy," etc.). This is a sign of our limited ability to register music, yes, but it has also become a means of wrongly turning music into a comprehensive, unified spectacle. Barthes notes that the adjective has "an economic function," meaning that it creates a tidy economy in our sense of the music, giving us a clear means of grasping its complex experience and holding on to it (178). Thus music is somehow neatly "constituted" (179). In so-called "classical music" (Barthes' focus again in this essay), the practice of applying adjectives gradually infiltrated the notations of the musical score itself, such that a "simple indication of tempo" like *allegro* (briskly, lively) is extended adjectivally to become a detailed mood. For example, one of Claude Debussy's piano pieces, "La Puerta del Vino" (The Wine Gate), includes the notation "Avec de brusques oppositions d'extrême violence et de passionnée douceur" (with sharp contrasts of extreme violence and passionate gentleness). As a result of such notations, a certain *"ethos"* of music comes to be asserted, and music "attributed a regular...mode of signification" (180). In other words, the adjective becomes a means of simplifying and ordering musical experience in a reductive way.

The search for "grain" attempts to counter this tendency, and Barthes begins by adapting a theoretical distinction developed by Julia Kristeva, between the "pheno-text and the geno-text" (181). The pheno-text essentially refers to the text viewed according to the rules of language—its structure, its generic conventions, linguistic syntax, and so on. We might say that "Introduction to the Structural Analysis of Narratives" viewed *Goldfinger* from the vantage point of the pheno-text, in discussing its mechanics, how the text works in some ideal sense. The geno-text, by contrast, is the text considered from the perspective of its material realization, how it generates different possibilities through reading or speaking. One of Kristeva's examples is the distinction between written Chinese (the pheno-text of the kanji) and spoken Chinese (the geno-text, requiring tonal modifications). So the *"pheno-song"* would consist of the set parameters of the score—"all the features which belong to the structure of the language being sung, the rules of the genre, the coded form of the melisma [flourishes or embellishments of notes], the composer's idiolect, the style of the interpretation" and so on (182). The adjectival dimensions of music, we may note, are part of the pheno-song. The *"geno-song,"* by contrast, is the performance, the materialization of the music: "the volume of the singing and speaking voice," for example, or the moment of production "where the melody really works at the language" (182). Again, this is where voice encounters language, or, to put it differently, where language systems meet bodies.

Barthes first explores the distinction with a thought experiment: imagine listening to a "Russian bass" singer—or, as he calls him, a "cantor" (181). We will hear the pheno-song, yes, but "something is there, manifest and stubborn," that goes beyond the pheno-song. We hear something from the "cantor's body, brought to your ears in one and the same movement from deep down in the cavities, the muscles, the membranes, the cartilages" (181). And the cantor's Russianness is important here too, for his native tongue implies certain practices of articulation specific to "the Slavonic language" (181). The point is not that this singer has a personal style: we are not trying to locate the personal idiom, the personality, the identity, of the individual here (182). What we are hearing, rather, is his "separate body," or specifically "the materiality of the body speaking its mother tongue" (182). Here we will find *"signifiance"* or, as it is called here, *grain* (182). Barthes develops this distinction further taking the example of two performers: the well-known German baritone Dietrich Fischer-Dieskau (1925-), whose extensive recordings were extremely popular, and Charles Panzéra (1896-1976), a less popular Swiss baritone. Fischer-Dieskau, "an artist beyond reproach," perfectly executes his performances, and expressively too. Yet his singing is more concerned with technical proficiency and clarity—"the emotive modes of its delivery" (183). In particular, he is known for the power of his lungs, the "discipline of breathing" (183), such that, listening to his performances, one only hears "the lungs, never the tongue, the glottic, the teeth, the mucous membranes, the nose" (183). Panzéra, by contrast, reveals the bodily dimensions of his performances. One hears the consonants, in his songs, as *"patinated*, given the wear of a language that had been living, functioning, and working for ages past" (184). One hears the lips forming certain vowel sounds, or the particular roll of the *r* deep in his throat (184). In short, one hears grain, one hears the body meeting language. Which of the two is more popular? Fischer-Dieskau, since French culture is wrongly committed to the simplified, streamlined pheno-song. It wants art to "be clear," to "'translate' an emotion and represent a signified" (185). Under the "tyranny of meaning," the institutional, official music of Fischer-Dieskau sets the parameters of how we hear music, thereby limiting our perceptions. "Panzéra does not belong to this culture," but in his marginal position represents an older form of music lost in consumer culture. In "Musica Practica," Barthes described the transition from the amateur performer to the specialized musical technician or "expert"; this transition had removed the insights of *musica practica* from our experience of music, transferring them to another. Here he offers a parallel argument: again, the consumerist music industry of polished recordings has privileged technical clarity, gradually suppressing the grainy singers of an earlier moment. Thus if one wants to listen to the songs of Schubert, one must listen to Fischer-Dieskau (185).

Barthes proceeds to develop another example that may be hard to follow if one is not familiar with the traditions of what is called "classical music." He speaks specifically of two competing song traditions, the German *lied* (associated here with Robert Schumann, but also the Russian composer Modest Mussorgsky) and the French *mélodie* (associated with Claude Debussy, Gabriel Fauré, and Henri Duparc). These two choral forms reflect broader attitudes about language in the respective poetic traditions, the German being more for reading, the French more for oratorical performance. What this means is that both French poetry and *mélodie* amount to "a practical reflection...on the language" (186). The difference here is *not* between a simple and straightforward singing of the song and an expressive interpretation—in fact, one should reverse the terms. The expressive and dramatic performance is precisely the approach to music that covers up the grain, by filling the performance with interpretive clues and affects that guide our perceptions. By contrast, the simpler performance may allow us to see the practice of language at work more clearly. So Barthes argues in contrasting two operatic death scenes, that of Boris in Mussorgsky's opera "Boris Godunov," and that of Mélisande in Debussy's opera "Pelléas et Mélisande." Boris's death song is *"expressive"* to the point of being *"hysterical,"* meaning it "is overloaded with historical, affective contents" (186). In this way it is aggressively pheno-song, regulating perception, and "smothering...*signifiance* under the soul as signified" (186-87). What is performed here is "passion *such as men speak and imagine it*, the accepted idea of death, *endoxical* death"—what is imagined as the orthodox death experience (187). By contrast, the death song of Mélisande, in the French opera is not overly expressive, it is only prosodic. "[N]othing occurs to interfere with the signifier," and what we encounter is "simply, the production of a music-language with the function of preventing the singer from being expressive" (187). Again, Barthes notes that the *lied* has won out over the *mélodie*, as mass music prefers the clarity of the former to the uncertain nuances of the latter (187). And he laments, "the French are abandoning their language, not...as a normative set of noble values...

but as a space of pleasure, of thrill, a site where language works *for nothing*" (187).

It may help to consider more contemporary musical examples. The French-Canadian superstar Céline Dion offers a good example of a singer of pheno-songs. Renowned for her tremendous voice, its strength and clarity, her performances (now regularly in Las Vegas) are heralded for their expressive execution and technical proficiency—a combination expressed in the term "power ballad." By contrast, we might consider an artist like the British P. J. Harvey as a performer of the geno-song. Many of her songs demonstrate her voice, her body, engaged with the English language—clipping consonants, punctuating or stretching words in unusual ways, or disrupting the conventions of song with lines that are too long or weak rhymes. The difference between Dion and Harvey is not one of "timbre" (185): it's not that Harvey modulates her voice in a way that Dion does not. Dion's songs are full of timbre, which is essential to her style of expressiveness. As Barthes writes, the crucial matter with timbre is what this "friction" in the voice indicates; if it conveys emotion to better send its "message," it is not grain, but if it rubs up against "the particular language" itself, we experience grain. One can think of any number of examples of geno-song and pheno-song singers, but the latter must be understood as calling attention to the act of language itself, not some emotional program. When Janis Joplin sings "O Lord, won't you buy me a Mercedes-Benz?" it is not the rasp of her voice or her slightly off-note singing that indicates grain, but rather the ways she plays with English, as in the collapse of words ("wontcha") or the deliberately "unrefined" pronunciation (the hard *r*, the quick rhythm) of "Mercedes-Benz"). In other words, it's not that she gives a performance with character, with a sense of her voice, but that she invites a larger reflection on language through her interpretation.

With the essay's final section, however, Barthes extends his discussion of grain beyond the sphere of vocal music, and clarifies the larger stakes of the concept. He imagines, for instance, extending consideration of grain to instruments, and how we hear the body interacting with them in different ways. Barthes discusses different modes of playing the piano, focusing on the grain of playing from the fingertips (189), but a more familiar example might be the contrast between clear trumpet playing in military music or trumpet concertos, and the very different, typically grainy style of jazz performances, where improvisation calls more attention to the body's interaction with the horn. Indeed, from the broader sense of musical grain, we could imagine "a different history of music" that, like the different history of the text (described in "From Work to Text") leaves genre behind altogether to focus instead on currents of grain—say, linking Panzéra's classical performances with Billy Bragg's singing. And to go still further, one could imagine the grain of "the hand as it writes, the limb as it performs" (188). Barthes had already hinted at this in looking at actors' faces and gestures in "The Third Meaning," or the play with French in Mallarmé's poetry (in "The Death of the Author"). We must always remember, however, that what we are describing is not "subjective," as many would perceive it. Our interest in grain is not about liking it, about having an opinion about what constitutes good performance. Our reaction to grain is bodily, "is erotic"; it is not our consciousness listening to the music, but our body (188). And our sensual response to the grain is not about "reinforc[ing]...the subject but, on the contrary,...los[ing] it" (188). Attention to grain is about recognizing an additional element of the human encounter with language—the bodily, sensual dimension in which language comes about, and where we find further resources in resisting the dominant unified meaning that our culture tries to impose on us.

13. Writers, Intellectuals, Teachers

In his first published book, *Writing Degree Zero* (1953), Barthes argued that the best literary writing was perpetually engaged in a struggle to express social speech. Speech was the sphere of both meaningful communication and an engagement with reality. Writing, by contrast, was "'closed' and thus different from spoken language."[7] Destined to obey certain formal conventions and the rules of style, the best writing constantly attempted to approximate or express the dynamism of speech, only to become sedimented and rigid over time. Albert Camus, for example, captured elements of everyday speech in works like *The Stranger* (1942), but his innovations, startling when his novels first appeared, quickly became a recognized style of literature. This dynamic was typical of literature more generally: it was always destined to remain remote from, falling short of, speech. We have seen how, across the 1960s, Barthes reversed this position on writing. As a complex arrangement of signifiers, writing came to be understood as "text," as a perpetually open sphere of meaning for the creative, active reader. By contrast, *speech*, once understood as dynamic,

---

7   *Writing Degree Zero*, trans. Annette Lavers and Colin Smith (New York: Hill & Wang, 1968), 19.

came to be understood as rigid and "irreversible" (190). It is with this problem that Barthes begins this last essay, published in the theoretical journal *Tel Quel* in 1971. The problem of this essay—posed by the title—concerns the different roles of a figure like Barthes himself. On the one hand, he was a teacher, conducting seminars, lectures, and classes in speech. On the other hand, he was a writer. These two functions meant that he was engaged in two different linguistic modes: writing, which he celebrated for its openness, and speaking, which he decried for its closure. Between these two positions, trying to mediate between them, was the intellectual, "the person who prints and publishes his speech" (190). The problem of the essay, then, is to explore how the intellectual reconciles these two roles and their corresponding modes of language. How can someone committed to the openness of writing engage in teaching? And how might one translate the rigid speech of teaching into meaningful writing? "Writers, Intellectuals, Teachers" attempts to explore such problems, and to do so in the form of twenty fragments. These fragments are a formal attempt to disrupt the steady flow of a teacher's lecture, by moving abruptly from one aspect of the problem to another. Our reading here will follow these different arguments.

Two constraints

Barthes opens the essay noting that there is "a (political) crisis in teaching" (190), which is specifically the question of the teacher's authority in the classroom. Is the teacher the voice of truth and authority? And if so, why? The first four fragments attempt to explain the position of the teacher, and the limitations she faces attempting to modify her position.

Barthes develops his argument about the dangers of speech here, noting first that it "cannot be *retracted*, except precisely by saying that one retracts it" (190). When the intellectual writes, she can change, delete, and modify words, but when the teacher teaches, everything she says remains said, and when she clarifies—by saying "*or rather…*" or "*I expressed myself badly…*"—she is simply adding to what has already been said. So while we may think that writing is "indelible" and unchangeable, and that speech is "ephemeral," the reverse is actually the case: the imprecisions or errors of speech cannot be unsaid, and writing (for the active reader) can always be modified and expanded (190-91). This makes the teacher something like a patient in psychoanalysis. In the model of the psychoanalytic talking cure developed by Sigmund Freud and expanded by Jacques Lacan, the patient talks about himself, on and on, adding more details and corrections and clarifications. Through this process, the patient will experience the discomfort of not being able to express himself perfectly and precisely, and in fact, this is how the unconscious finds expression. Thus Barthes argues that "a chain of augmentative corrections"—those additions and clarifications we frequently add to speech— make up "the favoured abode of the unconscious part of our discourse" (191).

Not only is speech something we cannot retract, but it is also something constrained by a very narrow context. We may think of the dynamic of speech with reference to Barthes' analysis of the narrative in "Introduction to the Structural Analysis of Narrative," or his discussion of the film in "The Third Meaning." Remember that in those essays Barthes stresses horizontal and vertical forms of signifying. The temporal flow of the film, or the constant forward movement of the narrative, drive the viewer or reader through time, unable to stop and perceive different modes of meaning. This is why the movie still is so important—we stop the film to perceive the signifiance of a potential "third meaning" in an image. Likewise, the active reader may resist the narrative's forward movement (by stopping and dwelling on a page, or by reading a passage at random). Speech is like the narrative or the film in its forward movement. If one is teaching, one must keep on going, "like a cyclist or a film" (191). One cannot stop, and if one pauses, the "[s]ilence and vacillation" create a sense of discomfort or impatience in the class. And as one keeps on talking, one is therefore preventing the proliferation, the "polysemy," of meaning (191).

These "two constraints"—the irretrievability of language and its constant temporal context in which language must keep on moving—limit the options for the teacher, who may define her position along a spectrum between two extremes. The teacher may decide that she will weigh her words carefully and speak with the clarity of polished, authoritative sentences, or she may instead pursue the hysterical attempt to clarify one's words. Such is the teacher who "chooses in all good faith a role of Authority" (191). But ultimately the difference between these two roles—the clear authoritative teacher, and the constantly correcting and clarifying teacher—is minimal. The teacher, trapped in speech, always "serves the Law," for "*all speech is on the side of the Law*" (191). If she speaks with clarity, she is pronouncing sentences which affirm her authoritative position: Barthes says such sentences can be compared to "penal speech," like the "sentences" handed down by a judge (191). Thus the two options for the teacher are both "gloomy" (192). One can act like the consummate authority figure, always precise, "without hesitation, at the right speed" and come across as a stark embodiment of the Law, "a kind of policeman" (191-92). Or one can clarify and amend, "correcting, adding, wavering"—but in this case, one does not subvert the nature of speech, but rather comes across as a certain kind of "*liberal*" politician, weakly fumbling about in an effort to be "less disagreeable" in one's role (192).

The summary

Another feature of the teacher's speech is that "one can (one may) summarize it" (193). Indeed, French education included an activity of exactly this kind of "*text reduction*" (193), though the most common form of summary is undoubtedly the taking of notes, whereby students "cull" from the teacher's speech certain "scattered statements...or the gist of an argument" (193). Teachers, Barthes notes, find looking at their students' notes an unpleasant experience— it is like "contemplating [oneself] in a reduced state," as shriveled as a shrunken head (193). Why is the experience so horrible? Because even the complexities of such a limited form of language as speech—the details, nuances, adornments, clarifications, style, and inflection—are all removed (193). Such an exercise therefore puts the teacher in the same camp as a legislator, whose speeches may also be summarized in a type of "Western" discourse (193). By contrast, writing cannot be summarized without destroying what actually constitutes it *as writing*—"a certain practice of the signifier" (194).

The teaching relationship

In the section *"Two constraints,"* Barthes had likened the speech of teaching to the speech of the patient in psychoanalysis, and he develops that argument a bit further in this fragment. One would at first think that the teacher is to her students like the psychoanalyst is to her patient: the figure of analytical insight and intervention. But this is not the case, for in psychoanalysis, it is the *patient* who talks while the analyst listens, while in the classroom, the *teacher* talks while the student listens. Thus the real parallel is that between the teacher and "the person analysed" (194). What this means is a certain unease built into the teacher's position. The teacher must "speak, endlessly, in front of and for someone who remains silent," constantly *"put[ting] out* a discourse" while *"never knowing how that discourse is being received"* (194). In analysis, the patient relies on the intervention or commentary of the analyst to know how she is being perceived, but the teacher often does not even get that kind of response, and is "ever forbidden the reassurance of a definitive image...which would *constitute*" him or her (194). As a result, the teacher is something like Harpo Marx in a famous scene in "A Night at the Opera" (1935); the Marx Brothers, disguised as Russians with long beards, are called to give a speech. Harpo, the Marx Brother who never talks, instead drinks water, which, dripping on his fake beard, gradually makes it begin to fall off. So feels the teacher, who, despite his or her speech, feels not only mute, but as if "coming unstuck piecemeal in front of everybody" (194). The teacher may make some witty comment and receive some reassuring response—smiles from the class, for example—but then may "regret the hysterical drive" to present him- or herself in such a fashion; he or she may assume that such responses "come from imbeciles or flatterers," and may not be sincere (194-95). In sum, the teacher constantly seeks, even provokes, certain responses, but can never trust them, and certainly should not feel that he or she is more truthful through such gestures.

The similarity of the teacher and the psychoanalytic patient does not imply that students serve in the same role as the analyst, however. But this sense that the students are not speaking will have a similar effect: "when the teacher speaks to [her] audience, the Other is always there, *puncturing* his discourse" (195). Such, says Barthes, is "the cross borne in every public act of speech"—the speaker will be like one on "the analytic couch" (196). In psychoanalysis, the foundation for the talking cure relationship is the phenomenon of transference, whereby emotions associated with a particular experience are ultimately transferred, in a different context, to the analyst. This is why the analyst's silence is so important: the transference depends on the imprecision and vagueness of the analyst as a figure. What Barthes concludes, from his comparison, then, is that "the teaching relationship is nothing more than the transference it institutes" (196). What we *think* teaching is about—the passing on of knowledge and ideas, method and science—are actually "*left-overs*" from this basic transference process (196).

The contract

Despite the transferential nature of the classroom, Barthes notes that this space is nonetheless defined by "an implicit contract between the teacher and the taught" (196). The contract is "imaginary," in the sense that it is not explicit or codified, but it is nonetheless powerful. Overall, the contract concerns the relationship between the teacher and the student, as the former searches for employment and the latter fulfills the terms of her own employment. And here Barthes spells out some of the assumptions of this contract. On the teacher's side, there is an expectation that she will be acknowledged in her role as a teacher (as an authority about a certain kind of knowledge). There is the expectation that the students will "relay" the ideas of the classroom "far afield" (196). There is an expectation of a certain kind of "loving relationship," whereby the student agrees to be "seduced" by the nature of the educational experience (196). The teacher also expects the student to respect the teacher's own relationship with her employer and workplace, and therefore to respect the nature of the job (what she can or cannot do as an employee) (197). On the side of the student, there are contractual expectations as well. The student expects the teacher to provide "good professional training," and to "fulfil the roles traditionally devolving to the teacher," such as the passing on of crucial knowledge and cultural authority (197). The teacher is expected to "reveal the secrets" of certain techniques, like how best to take an exam, write an assignment, or read a text. More generally, the teacher should provide instruction in the methods and fundamentals of learning in general: in this sense, the teacher is expected to be a secular "*guru*" of sorts (197). The teacher is also expected to represent a particular position or cause, and to "be its spokesman"—one can imagine the expectations on Barthes to represent the ideas of structuralism or post-structuralism (197). Relatedly, the teacher should admit the student to the special language of that movement (197). If the student has a particular project or idea she wants to pursue, the teacher should "guarantee the reality of that fantasy" as part of the educational process (197). And finally, the teacher will perform certain tasks (signing forms, or writing letters of recommendation) (197).

Why does Barthes mention this contractual side of teaching? As several later fragments will demonstrate as well, the left student movement of the 1960s had challenged precisely the corporate and contractual nature of education, both for the authority it afforded teachers and for the way it packaged education as a commodity for employment. Many radicalized students therefore sought to disrupt the classroom contract in various ways. Barthes discusses some of these more explicitly in *"The destruction of stereotypes," "In the name of what?,"* and *"Familiarity,"* among other fragments, and as we will see, this essay is an attempt to challenge the official status of the teacher. But here he quotes Bertolt Brecht once again, and to the effect that contracts provide security for parties in a "reciprocal relationship" (196). Barthes agrees with this view, and concludes the fragment by asserting that the best tactic for students and teachers is to "accept philosophically the plurality of their [contractual] determinations" (197). They should do this because "the truth of a relationship of speech is *elsewhere*" (197). That is, if one accepts the contract, one can most effectively ignore it. For it is not the contract that is the problem, but rather the authoritative nature of speech that he has been criticizing.

Research

With this fragment, Barthes begins to turn more to the problem of the relationship between the three vocational labels of his title, here the connection between the writer and the intellectual engaged in "research." What exactly is "research"? What is the result of research—is it a definable thing "one wants to find" (197)? How we answer that question obviously depends on one's discipline, but for anyone working with texts, the "'result' is *im-pertinent*"— simply not pertinent—says Barthes (198). How is this so? How might results not be pertinent to research? Barthes is not talking only about literary scholars interpreting prose or poetry; he insists on a broader understanding that includes any scholar interpreting language. In such instances—most cases of research—the intellectual's study also takes a linguistic form, specifically that of writing. Indeed, "'[r]esearch' is then the name which prudently... we give to the activity of writing," which makes research "an adventure of the signifier" (198). Given the nature of writing explored in the other essays of *Image-Music-Text*, one therefore cannot equate "research" with the "result" (198). That is, the significance of research is not some result we can summarize, but the process of searching and producing understanding through writing. As Barthes says, "whatever [research] searches for, it must not forget its nature as language" (198).

In other words, what Barthes is describing in this fragment is the conflicted way we understand research, which captures some of the tensions inherent in writing. Remember his assessment of the narrative in "Introduction to the Structural Analysis of Narrative": he argued that some parts of the narrative (the horizontal movement through time, for example) create a sense of progression and completeness, while others (the vertical integrative elements, for example) highlight the messiness and multiplicities of language. So it is with the writing of research. If we sense a "productive, dissatisfied, progressive, critical element...ordinarily granted to 'research,'" we are sensing these different tendencies in language. We are sensing how the process of meaning works, but also how that process is obscured. Herein lies the misunderstanding of research—researchers think they are *speaking*, that their language is clear, that they produce results, but they are actually writing, immersed in language, engaged in a messy process of production. In the terms of this essay's title, the intellectual is actually a writer, but often thinks of herself as a teacher. Could researchers be clear about their writing, the idea of their discipline would be fundamentally "changed" (198). The intellectual would be more clearly on the side of the writer, as too might the teacher.

The destruction of stereotypes

With this fragment, Barthes returns to the classroom setting, and becomes more explicit in addressing the question of teaching's "(political) crisis" (190). He begins with the anecdote that he has heard about a group of leftist students who are "preparing a destruction of the structuralist myth" (198). Here we should recall the argument of "Change the Object Itself," in which Barthes argued that myth-debunking had become a myth in its own right: the idea of the debunker trying to get at an underlying truth was itself mythical and stereotypical. Barthes repeats this argument, noting that such students embody a "stereotypic consistency" as predictable as "revolutionary students" or "war widows" (198). Such a stereotype is both ridiculous and sad, "at once corny and solemn": one resorts to stereotypical roles as an alternative to thinking about the complexities of language (199). One prefers the political clarity of the stereotype, which allows one to assume a "political discourse" in which the answers are pre-determined: as such, the stereotype is a "form of opportunism" in which one opts for the power of the stereotype rather than the work of criticism in and through language (199). One's efforts to keep this "stereotype at a distance" are important precisely because the stereotype implies a simplistic and false view of language—what Barthes calls "'natural' language" (199). Worse, when one adopts stereotypes," one is taking sides with the dominating aspects of language, specifically the repressive forms of language inherent in teaching and speaking. If one takes the complexities of language seriously, one cannot resort to such political simplifications, but must attack the discourse of stereotypes "like an acid" (199). Language is neither "mechanistic" nor the "mere response to stimuli of situation or action" (199). We must think not about language's "simple and fallacious utilization," but "the production of language" (199). Put most simply, the student de-bunkers, in wanting to attack a specific discourse (structuralism), err in assuming a simplistic view of language, which puts them precisely on the side of the authoritative language they seem to want to challenge. In challenging the teacher, they are on the side of teaching, not writing.

The chain of discourses

The preceding fragment concluded by asking if one should try to "'transcend' stereotypes [like 'revolutionary students'] instead of 'destroying' them" (199). The question here assumes a fantasy of dialectical thinking often associated with the German philosopher Georg W. F. Hegel, specifically the view that ideas develop in a mappable progression. The classic version of dialectics maintains that a "thesis" is countered by an opposing position or "antithesis," and then is resolved on a higher level or transcendent solution—the "synthesis." In the example of student revolutionaries wanting to destroy structuralism, Barthes' critique would be the antithesis, or opposing argument. Could one then hope for a transcendent solution then—say, students critiquing the idea of the teacher? Barthes answers in the negative, because in his view, dialectical thinking simply does not exist. One can see why Barthes would be skeptical of this view of dialectics. His focus on writing, texts, and signifiers, rather than on authors, works of pure ideas, and signifieds, means that he is skeptical of the notion of great thinkers moving abstractly from denotation to denotation, idea to idea. If ideas are always expressed in writing, then what we take to be dialectics must be something else. This fragment tries, then, to give an alternative view of dialectical thinking.

Let us look at another example—that of the progression of the field of linguistics. Bloomfieldian behaviorism is countered by Chomskyan mentalism, which is then challenged by a new semiotics (200). We would seem to see here a confirmation of dialectical theory. But Barthes points out that Chomsky's response to the new semiotics is *not* to incorporate these new theories into his viewpoint, in some kind of synthesis, but rather to "*jump* over his immediate predecessors" and return to grammatical theory from seventeenth-century France. This is not "dialectics," but rather a movement through discourses focused on "*clashes*" against prevailing dominant ideas, or "*doxa*" (200). More precisely, a new discourse emerges not as a "synthesis" in some orderly dialectical movement, but because writing works away at the prevailing *doxa*, finding "difference, distinction, working loose *against* what sticks to it" (200). In other words, new discourses are literally *paradoxical*, moving around (para-) the established ideas (-doxa) (200). This is true, as well, of an intellectual profoundly associated with dialectics, Karl Marx. "Marx's discourse is almost entirely *paradoxical*," his writing defined not by a transcendence of preceding ideas, but resisting and critiquing dominant ideas, like those of the socialist Proudhon, for example (200).

What Barthes offers, then, as an alternative to dialectics is the image, taken from the Italian political theorist Giambattista Vico (1668-1744), of the *spiral*. The spiral coil shows the "*drift* of circularity," the way ideas move around other ideas in the dynamics of writing. To understand an intellectual, one must not search for what is being synthesized, but rather what *doxa* is being challenged or corrected. With this observation, Barthes can conclude with a nod toward the problem of teaching. One could usefully evaluate teaching "in terms of paradox," looking at it as a "system calling for corrections, translations, openings, and negations" (200). In this way, one might begin to redeem the position of the teacher, and understand the progression of discourses, without the simplified fantasy of dialectics.

Method

Just as dialectics serves as a structuring fantasy for intellectuals, so too does "method," the term we give to the guiding principles of intellectual work. Method stands as a kind of "Law," the decisive key that some people desperately seek. It seems to be a "meta-language," a language about how language and ideas work, but Barthes insists that proclamations about method are "ultimately sterile" (201). Why? Because all the power of methodological work is focused on what texts should be, rather than on doing what texts do: methodological declarations "kill a piece of research," and guarantee that "the text never comes" (201). As a result, method speaks in a distorted way to only one of the "two demands to which the work of research must reply" (201). On the one hand, we demand of research "lucidity" and clarity, a discussion of "a procedure" and its "implications," and a "*critique*" of the ideas the research is supposed to engage and challenge (201). But at the same time, we seek from research a place of "writing," a "space of dispersion of desire," and the dismissal of Law (201). That is, we demand that research do the things that writing does. Method speaks to the clarity we demand of research, but at the expense of the explorations of writing. Therefore, we must "turn against Method" or "treat it without any founding privilege," as one "*view*" possible within writing (201). To put it in the terms of "From Work to Text," we demand that method be at once work (clear and established) *and* text (creative and multiple), but we only get the former, at the expense of the latter.

Questions

In this fragment, Barthes explores another basic concept that we associate with intellectual work, the question. We assume that questions are basic to the pursuit of knowledge: if an intellectual presents her ideas, the resulting questions will be devoted to better understanding, clarification, and more generally the pursuit of greater meaning. A question, we imagine, implies a "lack"—the questioner still does not understand something, and wants more information. In fact, this is not how many questions work, and Barthes gives the example of the intellectual's presentation that is followed by questions that are really attacks or challenges. If someone asks *"What's the use of linguistics?,"* the question is not really asking about linguistics and how it may be used; rather, it is implying that linguistics is ridiculous and not helpful, and the intellectual is wasting his or her time with it (202). In this scenario, however, the intellectual cannot answer, "Why are you attacking me?" (202) or "Why are you so opposed to linguistics?" Instead, one must conform to the fantasy of questions-and-answers, and respond as if the question is sincere and serious. In other words, "[w]hat I receive is the connotation"—the implied meaning of the question evident in the structure of the question, the style of its delivery, and so on, but "what I have to return is the denotation"—that is, I have to respond to the question as if its meaning is clear and straightforward (202). It is this trap—whereby one has to act like the question is serious—that sustains the dialectical fantasy: such exchanges, says Barthes, are the "masks of the dialectical relationship" (202). So while much of intellectual discourse is the clashing of ideas and the refusal to listen, it nonetheless "always gives itself 'natural' airs," claiming "to exchange only signified, not signifiers" (202).

In the name of what?

Barthes has argued that a methodological form of discourse is false in that it tidies up writing and makes it seem clearer than what it is. This fragment, however, begins the exploration of how one might write about one's own writing or speech. For Barthes has written himself into a contradiction of sorts. He has criticized speech for its false clarity, instead privileging writing for its creative multiplicity. Yet here he is, writing about speech. Given his speech-writing distinction, how can his writing about speech be clear? Barthes concedes he is trapped in this contradiction, "denounc[ing] the imaginary of speech through the irreality of writing" (203). Barthes' answer to this puzzle is to concede that he is not "giving the picture of any 'real' teaching" in his writing, for all he can do is "tell the truth on language" without telling "the truth on the real" (203). To return to this fragment's opening question, then, "in the name of what" is Barthes writing? Barthes' answer enacts the contradiction he recognizes: "I speak only in the name of a language" (202). Note that Barthes says he *speaks* rather than *writes*: as he clarifies, he "speak[s] because [he has] written," and "writing is represented by its contrary, by speech" (202). In short, we cannot clearly distinguish writing and speech in this essay, which is rather an attempt to approximate different types of language.

The standing position

This fragment imagines the scenario of speaking before an audience in which some listeners are uncomfortably seated or, worse, standing. In such a situation, one might wonder whether the exchange—the discomfort of standing is the price of the speaker's words—is worthwhile. One may reasonably doubt that one's words are worth it, in which case one might imagine that the "standing position" captures a feeling of "*un-ease,*" a position that is "eminently *critical*" (203). But the point of the fragment is not about this particular scenario but what it might represent. It is Barthes' way of imagining a more productive dynamic in the classroom. For paying attention to the listener in the "standing position," one can begin to imagine how the exchange of language might seem legitimate or worthwhile. Specifically, the speaker must learn first the "vanity of [his or her] own speech," and then begin to think about the "circuit of exchange" (203). In this way, the speaker can begin to think about him- or herself as the listener to whom the speech is addressed.

Familiarity

In French, there are two forms for the pronoun "you": the plural "vous" and the singular "tu." But in French, the "vous" form is also used in formal situations, while the "tu" form is used among close friends and for people much younger than the speaker. Student radicals of the late 1960s, however, began using the "familiar *tu*-form" in speaking to their teachers (203). What is happening when this occurs? Barthes believes this is an assertion of "signifieds," whereby the student asserts "militancy or mateyness—*muscle*"—in speech with a supposed superior. A "morality of the sign is here imposed," as the student insists on his or her equality and familiarity with the teacher (203). The problem with such familiarity is that it asserts an attitude toward language without taking language seriously. If one wants to explore signs, if one wants to assess one's interlocutor and determine what kind of person she is, one must remain in the more "neutral ground" of the formal "vous" form. By refusing to remain in this more neutral space, the familiar student is simplifying language, "shift[ing] toward the operational," and therefore shutting down analysis (203-4). The student gives up on the interpretive complexity of the situation, and opts instead for a shortcut, the "tu" form. For this reason, familiarity is a form of "flight" or evasion of engagement. Again, the issue here is less the particular scenario than the larger principle, for Barthes is not concerned with the disrespect that a few students show to teachers. The larger issue here is the "shift of this kind" that often happens in language, when, say, political discourse ceases to examine and resorts to a simplified shorthand principle (204).

An odour of speech

This is another fragment in which Barthes tries to comment on this essay as a piece of writing without becoming methodologically prescriptive. He begins with the metaphor of smell in relation to speech, saying that when "one has finished speaking, there begins the dizzying return of the image" (204). One turns over the experience of speech in one's memory, regretting or exalting it. For this reason, one might say that speech "*smells*"—that is, it leaves behind a trace with a particular sense, or odor. By contrast, writing comes and goes: it may "*travel* far from my body" and if so it "*falls*...like a meteorite disappearing" (204). A speaker will dwell on his or her speech, but rarely does the writer dwell on his or her words to the same degree. In a sense, then, Barthes imagines speech to be something solid, leaving a trace (that could be compared to a scent), while writing is something more gaseous, ethereal, dispersed. Let us leave aside whether we agree with this, and consider the basis for the distinction. Barthes believes that, with speech, we always recall the situation or context of the speaking, which is why we can recall our verbal comments so well; writing, by contrast, "has no past," by which he means that no such authoritative position accompanies our recall (204).

With this written analysis, Barthes shifts, in the third paragraph, to further parenthetical musings about this essay. He wonders why "this present text preoccupies" him—if it is a piece of writing, why is he so concerned with it, as if it is speech (205)? His answer is that the "very status of the piece" is contradictory; for while he tries to "liquidate" speech, to empty it of its negative linguistic force, he cannot do so *in writing itself*" (205). The problem, more precisely, is that in writing his critique of speech, he constantly tries to evoke "illusions of experiences, memories, and feelings had by the subject I am when I speak," and as a result, his writing evokes the stink of speech (205). We may read this parenthetical paragraph as an admission that the clear distinction between speech and writing does not hold fast, but is a fiction that Barthes is developing for the purposes of his argument. As he wrote in *"The chain of discourses,"* all writing must proceed in a *paradoxical* manner, circling and spiraling around a *doxa*. This is what he is doing in "Writers, Intellectuals, Teachers," and in calling attention to the contradiction, he is inviting readers to critically assess his success, rather than naively follow his argument.

Our place

If we imagine the classroom spatially, we might envision an authoritative space at the front for the teacher, and subordinate spaces in the back for the audience of students. It might therefore be like that space we imagine in a Christian church, in which a priestly figure stands in the elevated pulpit over the flock of parishioners. This is how we might also understand "the past" as a higher space speaking to us below, in the present (205). In other words, we can spatially map discursive spaces in terms of highs and lows, and the uneven authority granted to some at the expense of others. Such an exercise reminds us that our notions of language are often spatial, and that the correct problem to pose is not who gets to stand above or before everyone else, nor how to "abolish the distinction in functions" like teacher and student, nor even how we can rearrange and reimagine the space of language (206). With speech environments (like the classroom), the challenge, rather, is to "protect the instability" of "the positions of speech" (206). Here the problem of speech must be reoriented away from the nature of speech itself (its authoritative quality) to spaces in which the positions of speech remain unfixed and therefore disruptive of speech. In the classroom, the teacher may always have a "fixed place" at the outset, but our goal is to start the discourse moving about the room in the production of some kind of *"excess"* (206).

We should note a few things about this fragment. First of all, it more or less rejects the starting premise of the essay— that speech is a negative and dominating form of language as opposed to writing—in suggesting that there is a movement and instability of speech positions that can be developed and encouraged. Why this contradiction? A simple answer might be that Barthes wants to figure out how the classroom space might function differently than the church-like norm. But if we consider the shift in his argument, we may see it less as a contradiction and more as a demonstration of one of this essay's principles: that writing allows for a shifting of positions (here, the changing position on speech) through the process of writing around a problem (the paradoxical nature of writing described in *"The chain of discourses"*). What we are witnessing, as we read these fragments, is the movement and gradual mutation of Barthes' argument, as if to demonstrate how writing can generate new positions.

Two types of criticism

The next three fragments focus on problems of intellectual activity, or frameworks of analysis—criticism, discourse, and the axiomatic field. Here we will see Barthes attempting, more than in any other piece in this collection, the formulation of a new political position that speaks to his two interests: psychoanalysis and marxism (also the topic of *"Our unconscious"* and *"Writing as value"*).

The first of these fragments begins with another seemingly trivial anecdote: let us imagine the intellectual typing out a manuscript, and making a few errors. The errors might be of two types: first, a word might be so misspelled that the mistake has no meaning—one types out "offiver" instead of "officer"; second, a word might be mistyped as another word—one means to type "rude" but instead types "ride" (206). From these two mistakes, one can extrapolate two different kinds of criticism. In the first instance, which Barthes calls *"signifiosis"* (207), the critic celebrates the error's resistance to meaning, explores new associations of meaning, and makes attempts to explode the text in different directions as she wishes, "making them into a new music" of sorts (207). In the second instance, which Barthes associates with *"signifiance,"* the critic still operates in the realm of mistaken words, but does so by tracing the "sliding *within the codes*—meaning remains but pluralized, cheated, without law of content, message, truth" (207). The first kind of criticism "supposes a utopian vision of freedom" in which the critic does what she will with writing: there are no restraints, no limits, just the free play of associations (207). "[T]he law is lifted *all at once*, outside of any history, in defiance of any dialectic," but risks degenerating into the "disorder" of "hysterical rambling" (207). Outside of any constraints, "it is ultimately *my* reading which I impose," my "subjectivity" which I express (207-8). The second kind of criticism, however, is constrained by meaning, and consequently takes up "the division of meanings and the 'trickery' of interpretation," examining a "society locked in the war of meanings" (208). This kind of criticism entails what Barthes calls "semantic enterism," a metaphor he takes from politics, where enterism describes the tactic of joining a political party in order to change it from within.

Which of these two forms of criticism does Barthes prefer? Barthes' essays before this point have been ambivalent on this question. There are those places where Barthes celebrates the explosive power of the signifier and the generation of new meanings, and in this respect he would seem to prefer the first mode of criticism. But he has also stressed the need to undermine the rigidity of certain forms of (especially western) language from within language, and his earlier reflections on method and dialectics—that one must chip away at the doxa rather than assert some new position—means that he will come down here on the side of the second form of criticism. As he writes here, the second criticism is "more historically correct" because it seeks to remain engaged with language, rather than simply asserting some different linguistic sphere. This position is consistent, too, with his skepticism about debunking and destroying language. "Ideological criticism," he writes, must perform a kind of "theft," picking away at the signified from within the "*illusion* of meaning" (208).

Two types of discourse

In this fragment, Barthes comes close to repeating his argument about speech in the first fragment on "*Two constraints.*" His focus here is upon two different modes of discourse, "terrorist" and "repressive," the latter of which he also calls "liberal." We might imagine "terrorist" discourse to be that of "peremptory assertion…of a faith, a truth, a certain justice" (208)—in other words, a strong insistence on a set of values. In fact, a terrorist discourse is simply committed to the view that language is, can be, and should be always clear and "lucid"; in this way, it expresses the most violent dimensions of language, the idea that the "utterance" is able directly to express the truth (208). One might thus have a full-fledged terrorist discourse of clear "enunciation" (208), or "small-scale terrorisms" in the form of certain rhetorical tropes that posit clarity and self-evidence. The earlier-discussed use of the familiar "tu" form of language would be an example; this simple use of a pronoun implies a full set of seemingly clear positions about language and authority, for example. To this terrorist discourse we might oppose a more equivocal form of language, in which balances (either this or that, neither this nor that) are articulated, or in which the discourse does not seem to come down on a clear position but suggests a range of possible positions. This "liberal" discourse, however, must be understood as "repressive," for, whatever its nuances and clarifications, it is still outlining that spectrum "between what is forbidden and what is permitted, between commendable meaning and unworthy meaning" (209). Such a discourse will *appear* to be "*impartial*" and "*objective*," but is also spelling out the range of possible positions that are allowed (209).

The two discourses thus correspond to the two types of speakers mentioned in "*Two constraints*," the clear authoritative speaker (of terrorist discourse) and the equivocating, clarifying speaker (of liberal discourse). Has Barthes simply repeated an argument already made? Yes and no. Yes, this argument is extremely similar to the earlier one, but we must remember that the earlier claim stresses two types of speakers, while this fragment focuses on two types of discourses, which might be written as well. What Barthes is now describing is not the opposition between speech and writing, but rather tendencies in language more generally that go beyond the problem of speech and writing. This fragment thus stands as a clarification, an expansion, and even a correction of the earlier fragment, now shifting our attention away from the celebration of writing and the condemnation of speech to a more nuanced view of trends within intellectual discourses. In this way, Barthes is demonstrating the drift of language—its ability to correct itself, expand, clarify—as he revises earlier arguments. We might even say that the earlier claim was "terrorist" in nature, and in challenging the stark opposition between speech and writing, Barthes has shifted his discursive position.

The axiomatic field

This fragment, more than any other, engages with marxist politics, specifically beginning with a claim made by Bertolt

Brecht: "All that is necessary...is to determine those interpretations of facts appearing within the proletariat engaged in the class struggle (national or international) which enable it to utilize the facts for its action. They must be synthesized in order to create an axiomatic field" (209). Brecht's notion here is that critique for the working-class struggle against capitalism should be assembled from all the related facts and their interpretations; these axioms, or basic truths, can best be preserved and mobilized when arranged as a sort of force field to which the proletariat can always refer. Barthes takes this claim as problematic for several reasons. For one thing, it assumes that we can clearly characterize a fact's interpretation as bourgeois-capitalist or proletariat, as if language is as clearly divided as society (210). But a deeper problem is that many facts in our time do not seem to have proletarian interpretations—in an age of mass consumer culture, the proletariat may simply have no clear interpretation of phenomena that are widespread and not class-specific. There may not be, for example, clear proletarian positions on the World Cup, U2, *Trainspotting*, or the "latest news item" (210). In such instances, there may be intellectuals who serve the working class by providing them with "the proletarian interpretation of cultural facts" (210). But these "procurators"—intellectuals, like Barthes, who want to interpret on behalf of workers—have a problem: not only are they not proletarian, but they find their critical tools in the bourgeoisie they are supposedly criticizing (210-11). "Historicism, sociologism, positivism, formalism, psychoanalysis"—all are "bourgeoisified" (211).

The more serious problem, however, is that an axiomatic field simply does not exist. It is not as if there are set positions and interpretations that one can always apply, because the criticism of culture "proceeds *successively, diversely and simultaneously*" through different tactics (211). At one point it might counter "historicism with sociologism," while at another point, it might oppose "historicism with formalism"—that is, the tactic will always change depending on the context (211). For this reason, cultural critique will always be "a tissue of elements now past, now circumstantial...now finally and frankly utopian" (211). Tactics must always change, and furthermore one must keep in mind the ideal that one is trying to reach, the moment when the class war "comes to an end" (211). Accordingly, Barthes argues that in marxism, "all the discourses" he has listed "are present in its writing," including self-justification, the effort to destroy oppressive bourgeois culture, and the utopian formulation of how things should be in the future (211-12). Marxism cannot therefore be understood as a field of axioms, but as the dynamic of writing described in "The Death of the Author" and "From Work to Text": a field of different linguistic and rhetorical modes and positions operating from multiple perspectives. Politically, then, marxists must attempt not the clarification of rules and positions (the axiomatic field) but a field of multiple strategies and modes.

Our unconscious

This fragment takes up the corresponding problem of psychoanalysis, with reference to the work of the French psychoanalyst and theorist Jacques Lacan (1901-1981), a contemporary of Barthes. Sigmund Freud had stressed the importance of the unconscious to understanding human behavior, and Lacan, influenced by the same theories of language that inform Barthes' work, had argued that the unconscious must not only be structured like a language, but existed within the field of language, not in some private, completely individualized unconsciousness in the mind. If we ask "what is the relation between class determination and the unconscious" within a Lacanian framework, then, we must answer this question by assessing the class nature of language itself. One might argue, for example, that the working-class's unconscious, which exists in social discourse, is comprised of "bourgeois language... which speaks unconsciously in the proletariat's cultural discourse" (212). That is, the unconscious content of the working class, in a culture of bourgeois language, must be bourgeois. But at the same time, one might make a reverse argument: that the intellectual's unconscious is shaped and defined by the proletariat, even if proletarian culture is consciously secondary to the intellectual (212). What Barthes argues, then, is that our conscious use of language may be consistently troubled by an unconscious formulation of language from a different class. This may be one of the weakest of Barthes' fragments—the basis for the inverse class relationship is never made clear, but is rather asserted as an interesting possibility—but we may take this fragment as a speculation in the same vein as many of the other fragments. That is, it attempts to break down an analytical framework to imagine linguistic and discursive splits and how they might operate. Here the basic argument is that class conflict is structured within language itself, as the working class's discursive unconscious is bourgeois, while the non-proletarian intellectual's unconscious may be bourgeois.

Writing as value

One always inevitably criticizes from a point of evaluation—
something one values or holds dear—and for Barthes that
starting evaluation is the power of "writing" as he has
come to define it across the essays in *Image-Music-Text*.
Barthes is aware that this view of writing will strike many
as mystified and obscure—having a *"mystique"*—but
in this penultimate fragment he insists that his view is
"materialist" (213). We may remember Barthes' initial
problem, in his essays on photography, where he wanted
to explore how words might match up with the image of
reality. His conclusion was that there was an inevitable
gap between the denoted and the connoted, between the
signifier and the signified, such that we could not access
the material reality captured by photographic technology.
His subsequent essays began to shift the framework of
analysis to the signifier, finding in the signified—the rigid
view of language as a set system—a domination of thought
and freedom that needed to be challenged. One had to
pursue the signifier, significance, the process of meaning,
in opposition to the tendency of language to give the false
sense of products, things, and established meanings. As
opposed to the clear voice, one would focus on the grain of
meaning's production; as opposed to the clearly structured
narrative, one would focus on how meaning is constructed
within, and the interpretive possibilities evident in that
construction; as opposed to the fixed author figure or
the established idea of the work, one would focus on the
criss-crossing of discourses in the text as the reader engages
it; as opposed to the debunking of myths in the pursuit of
the thing, one would focus on undermining the rigidity of

signs themselves; as opposed to the unidimensional viewing of theater or films, one would stop their steady movement and focus on the dynamics of construction. In all of these instances, one's challenge was not to make language better correspond to reality (as in the earliest essays) but to shift the focus on language as the reality around us, rather than the marker of the reality beneath it. In this respect, the turn to language was the turn to reality itself, and an appreciation of the process and dynamics of language—which would be most evident in *writing*—would be our best chance to think about the reality around us, which is fundamentally linguistic but in a fluid sense. Thus the focus on writing "rejects the temptation of the signified" or static meaning, and resists a view of speech in its narrowest sense (213). Writing is *atopical*—that is, it does not fixate itself on particular abstractions. It is dispersed, beyond the immediate situation, like reality itself. In this sense, the linguistic focus on writing is truly materialist, while the fixation on set things is abstract and idealist.

Peaceable speech

As we have seen, Barthes' ideas about speech and teaching evolve across these fragments, and this last one concludes with a utopian view of the classroom as a seminar of open communication. Again, he begins with a seemingly simple, almost trite, problem: "*goodwill*," specifically in a "space of discourse divested of all sense of aggressiveness" (213). While it might seem that anyone would want a space of "goodwill," Barthes notes that many speakers resist a space devoid of linguistic aggression or violence. Some see goodwill as a mask for politeness, a bourgeois humanist lie masking real power relationships. Others find the absence of "conflictual discourse" to be "frustrating," assuming that greater understanding comes through the clash of dialogue. Others relatedly believe that aggressive discourse is necessary to splinter consensus, "in order that its contradictions may emerge" (214). All of these impulses, however, preserve "the unity of the neurotic subject, which *comes together* in the forms of conflict" (214). That is, the speaker feels whole and unified, like a solid person, through conflict. We see here another modification of Barthes' earlier critique of speech, which he initially found intrinsically aggressive: here the problem is the speech relationship and its space, a position he has come to through his various fragments.

This insight suggests the reverse, then—namely, that in a sphere of speech devoid of harsh judgment, advocacy, or intimidation, a different sense of the subject would emerge. Specifically, a collective feeling of "*a certain generalization of the subject*" might emerge, whereby one's language belongs to a more general sense of community (214). Barthes compares this feeling to that of smoking marijuana (he adds that he does not!), with which "everything is relaxed" and "disarmed," and speech comes to seem ironic or detached, an exercise for greater understanding (215). In contrast to a gathering of drinkers, in which the alcohol solidifies a strong sense of self and aggression, in the gathering of marijuana smokers, there is a "*suspension*" of strong positions. It is this suspension of self and language, this effort to undermine centralized speech, that one should strive for in the "teaching space" (215). Such a suspension would not overturn speech's expression of "Law" so much as "disorientate" it (215). Indeed, all the contractual requirements of the teacher would remain, as would all the ideological and methodological demands on the intellectual, but they would now be *"floating"* (215).

"Writers, Intellectuals, Teachers" is a challenging piece if we read it as a coherent argument or essay. But as a reading of its fragments shows, this is not an essay in that sense. Its initial argument, pitting writing against speech, is modified, developed, and fundamentally challenged, so that the last fragment re-envisions classroom speech as a utopian sphere. Consequently, the best way to read this piece is as a different kind of intellectual activity, a moving around orthodox views (including Barthes' own opinions) in an effort to generate new ideas and hypotheses. This is less an "argument" supported by various points than a map of someone's speculative thoughts on a cluster of problems from different angles. This is typical of Barthes' writings in the final decade of his life, including *The Pleasure of the Text* (1973), *Roland Barthes* (1975), *A Lover's Discourse* (1977), and *Camera Lucida* (1980). Some of Barthes' final lectures at the Collège de France have been transcribed and published—*Comment Vivre Ensemble* [*How to Live Together*], lectures delivered in 1976-77, *The Neutral*, from lectures delivered in 1978, and *The Preparation of the Novel*, lectures delivered in 1978-79 and 1979-80—and these show a similar approach in the classroom. He has essentially abandoned the paradigmatic essay and lecture forms, and adopts a writing or speaking style of often disjointed speculations. To read these requires a different approach than we normally assume; if we typically want to find key arguments, we instead find reflections that open up topics, requiring readers to carry on the writing process.

Nonetheless, we find in all of these fragments a final version of arguments that Barthes has made through much of *Image-Music-Text*, whereby the restrictive, static, and narrow perspective of a cultural form (music, photography, the narrative, theater) can be expanded by the change of perspective. Much as our musical experience can be reinvigorated by a Beethovian sense of the construction of the complex musical piece, or our reading of Genesis can be opened by a focus on the fractures of the text, so too can the authoritarian side of speech and teaching be opened up by a new attention to space, the relationship of the speaker to others, and a better sense of the codes of intellectual work more generally. What we see, ultimately, is that "writing" emerges as the paradigm for all human activities, such that even our discussions can be refigured as a "lesson in writing."

Reading Across Barthes' Work

Because the essays in *Image-Music-Text* cover such a range of Barthes' career, readers should find many of his earlier, contemporary, and subsequent works more accessible. *Writing Degree Zero* (published in 1953, translated by Annette Lavers and Colin Smith, 1967) first raises the question of the differences between speech and writing. *Mythologies* (1957) shows Barthes at work on a range of examples from contemporary French culture; the English translation (Annette Lavers, 1972) somewhat depoliticizes Barthes' overall work, so readers should consult *The Eiffel Tower and Other Mythologies* (1979, translated by Richard Howard). Related essays also appear in *What is Sport?* (translated by Richard Howard, 2007). *Criticism and Truth* (1966, translated by Katrine Pilcher Keuneman, 1987) is something of a statement about what a theoretically-informed literary criticism should be, in reaction to conservative critics. *The Fashion System* (1967, translated by Matthew Ward and Richard Howard, 1983) is a challenging read, as it was written when Barthes was most engaged with giving semiotics a sharply scientific inflection. It gives a different sense of Barthes than *Mythologies*, though his focus—fashion magazines' presentation of women's clothing—is similar. More accessible essays are found in the collection *The Language of Fashion* (2006, translated by Andy Stafford). Barthes' interest in Japan is developed more fully in *Empire of Signs* (1970, translated by Richard Howard, 1975).

The 1970s saw the publication of a number of Barthes' major later works, many related to the problems discussed across *Image-Music-Text*. *S/Z* (1970, translated by Richard

Miller, 1975) presents a challenging but rewarding reading of the Balzac story referenced in "The Death of the Author"; the edition includes the Balzac story. *The Pleasure of the Text* (1973, translated by Richard Miller, 1976) attempts to describe a different, more bodily reading practice. *Camera Lucida* (1980, translated by Richard Howard, 1982) returns to the question of signification in photography. *A Lover's Discourse* (1977, translated by Richard Howard, 1978) is perhaps most akin to "Writers, Intellectuals, Teachers" in attempting a reading of lived behavior and experience, specifically in romantic relationships. The posthumously published lecture notes titled *The Neutral* (1977-78, translated by Rosalind E. Krauss and Denis Hollier) will provide some sense of Barthes' attempts to formulate a different kind of politics. *Roland Barthes by Roland Barthes* (1975, translated by Richard Howard, 1977) is more rewarding after reading across Barthes' works, and is an engaging attempt at intellectual critique and autobiography.

A collection of interviews with Barthes, *The Grain of the Voice* (1981, translated by Linda Coverdale, 1985) provides a readable reflection on Barthes' work. Louis-Jean Calvet's *Roland Barthes* (1990, translated by Sarah Wykes, 1995) is the best biography, although Andy Stafford's *Roland Barthes, Phenomenon and Myth: An Intellectual Biography* (1998) is a useful recent overview of Barthes' career. Annette Lavers' *Roland Barthes: Structuralism and After* (1982) is one of the best discussions of Barthes' overall work, while *Bringing Out Roland Barthes* by D. A. Miller (1992) nicely situates much of Barthes' work from the *Image-Music-Text* moment in relation to his sexuality. Jonathan Culler's *Roland Barthes* (1983) is very useful as well. Three more detailed collections of essays on Barthes are the Spring 1997 special issue on Barthes of *Nottingham French Studies*, edited by Diana Knight; the Spring 2008 special issue of *Nottingham French Studies* focused on *Mythologies*, edited by Douglas Smith; and *Photography Degree Zero: Reflections on Roland Barthes's Camera Lucida* (2009, ed. Geoffrey Batchen).

Index

Many of the terms listed below are used throughout the book, so to make the index more useful I have given the page numbers where these concepts are introduced and explained. In addition, because I stress connections between the different essays in the collection, I have included entries for all of them below. Numbers in bold indicate the pages directly covering the essay in question; other page numbers indicate discussions to contextualize that essay. [E. W.]

actants (characters as), 85–88
analogon, 15
anchorage, 29–30
Aristotle, 86

Bakhtin, Mikhail, 43
Balzac, Honoré, 111–14, 121–22, 138
Bataille, George, 133
Beethoven, Ludwig van, 124–27
Benveniste, Émile, 70
Bragg, Billy, 158
Brecht, Bertolt, 53–65, 146, 150, 167, 183–84
Bunraku, 145–51

Camus, Albert, 159
Cardinal nuclei, 74–78
Catalysers, 74–78
"Change the Object Itself",
    139–45, 150–52, 169
Characters *see* actants
Chateaubriand, François-René de, 132–33

Chomsky, Noam, 171
Connotation, 16–23
Critic, 120–21

"Death of the Author, The",
    1–2, **111–22**, 123, 128–31,
    135–37, 151, 158, 185, 193
Debussy, Claude, 152, 155–56
Denotation, 16–23
Diderot, Denis, 53–65
"Diderot, Brecht, Eisenstein",
    53–65, 123, 128–30, 132–33,
    145, 151
Diegesis, 30–31
Dion, Céline, 157
Dosse, François, 3
Dumas, Alexandre, 138

Eisenstein, Sergei, 38–65

Fetish, 58–59
Filmic, 50–51
Fischer-Dieskau, Dietrich,
    154–55

Flaubert, Gustave, 11, 138
Fleming, Ian (creator of James Bond), 73–100
Fragment, 52–53, 160
Freud, Sigmund, 6, 23, 161, 185
"From Work to Text", 100, 112, **129–39**, 140, 145, 151, 158, 173, 185
Functions, 72–74

Geno-song (and geno-text), 153, 157
Gest (Brechtian), 61–63
"Grain of the Voice", 124, 128, 144, **151–59**
Griemas, Algirdas, 83, 109–10

Haiku, 49–50
Harvey, P. J. 157
Heath, Stephen, 1
Hegel, G. W. F. 24, 171

Idiolect, 35–36, 153
Indices, integrational, 78–81
Informants, 78–81
Interdisciplinarity, 131
Intertextuality, 135
"Introduction to the Structural Analysis of Narrative", 1, **65–100**, 104, 111–12, 114, 130, 134, 139, 153, 161, 168

James, Henry, 91
Joplin, Janis, 157

Kristeva, Julia, 4, 42, 153

Lessing, Gotthold, 60

Lévi-Strauss, Claude, 68, 71, 83
Lacan, Jacques, 4, 161, 185–86
"Lesson in Writing", **145–51**

Mallarmé, Stéphane, 116–18
Marx, Harpo, 164
Marx, Karl, 172
Marxism, 3–5, 10, 130, 136, 143, 180–85
Method acting, 62, 147–48
Mythologies, 4–12, 34, 70, 140–43, 192
"Musica Practica", **122–29**, 131–32, 137–38, 145, 151, 155
Mussorgsky, Modest, 155–56

Narration, 90–96
Network, 136–37

Panzéra, Charles, 154–55, 158
Paradox, 25, 51, 59, 107, 133, 172, 178, 180
Perspective, 88–90
Pheno-song (and phenol-text), 153, 157
"Photographic Message, The", **13–25**, 27, 31–33, 35, 37–38, 129, 144
Poe, Edgar Allan, 71
Pregnant moment, 60–61
Proletariat, 184–86
Propp, Vladimir, 74, 87, 109–10
Proust, Marcel, 117, 138
Psychoanalysis, 6, 40, 130, 161, 164–65, 184–85

Reader, 121–22

Relay, 15, 29–30, 83, 90
Representation, 56–57
"Rhetoric of the Image, The", **25–38**, 67, 77, 99
Romm, Mikhail, 47

Sartre, Jean-Paul, 91
Saussure, Ferdinand de, 6, 18, 68
Scriptor, 118–19
Semioclasm, 142–43
Sign, 6–10
Significance, 42, 180
Signification, 7–8
Signified, 6–10
Signifier, 6–10
Signifiosis, 180
Sociolects, 143–44
Speech, 159–65
Still (film), 51–52

"Struggle with the Angel", 1, **100–11**, 112, 119, 121, 130, 132, 134, 145
Surrealism, 117–18
Syntagm, 36–37

Tableau, 57–63
Text (vs. work) 130–31
Thibaudet, Albert, 133
"Third Meaning, The", **38–55**, 100–1, 129, 1233, 161–62
Todorov, Tzvetan, 67, 71, 83
Trauma, 21, 23

Valéry, Paul, 116–17
Vico, Giambattista, 172

Woolf, Virginia, 73
"Writers, Intellectuals, Teachers", 1, 3, 128, 145, **159–91**